THE WOOLLY AND THE BULLY OF THE WILD WEST

Strange Tales from the Cowboy Days

Stephen Shastay

*Learn this well, the last ride
is never the last ride. And
the end is not the end.*

Richard Rowland

CONTENTS

ELMER MCCURDY

The Bandit That Wouldn't Give Up

Poor Elmer McCurdy was a hapless loser. Luck was not his friend. Not during his life; not after he was dead. The best you can say about him is that he didn't give up. In fact, that became his nickname. He was "The Bandit Who Wouldn't Give up."

Elmer was born in Maine on January 1, 1880. His mother was Sadie McCurdy. His father was unknown, but some say he was Charles Smith, Sadie's cousin. The only proof of that is Elmer sometimes used Charles Smith as an alias.

Elmer grew up thinking he was the son of Sadie's brother, George, and his wife, Helen. Sadie told him the truth when he was a young teenager. She also told him that his father was unknown. Elmer started drinking. That was a habit he would continue for the rest of his life.

He worked as a plumber at first. Later he would be a miner in a lead mine. His work was fine, but he kept losing jobs because of his drinking. He spent three years in the Army. Part of his training was with nitroglycerin. Because of his future ineptitude with this particular explosive, it is suspected that he was not trained very well.

Elmer McCurdy

He was discharged on November 7, 1910. By November 19, Elmer and a buddy were in jail for possession of burglary tools. Somehow, they convinced the judge that they were using the tools in the creation of a foot-operated machine gun. They were released. Elmer immediately set out to rob banks and trains. Fumbling, bumbling Elmer was about to make his reputation.

McCurdy moved to Oklahoma and put his plans into action. His first train was the Iron Mountain-Missouri Pacific in March 1911. He heard rumors that the train would be carrying a safe with $4,000 in it. He got three friends to help him. They stopped the train. They found the safe. Elmer put his military training to work.

He brought nitroglycerin with him to the robbery. That in itself is very dangerous. He fixed up the nitro to blow the safe. There was a monstrous explosion, and the safe was opened. Well, it was opened in such a way that you could say it was destroyed. Elmer used too much nitroglycerin.

The paper money in the safe went up in smoke. Elmer and his crew had to settle for $450 in silver. Most of those coins had to be chipped off of the safe as the blast had melted and crudely welded them to the safe.

In September 1911, Elmer and two cohorts decided to rob The Citizens Bank in Chautauqua, Kansas. They spent a few hours breaking through a bank wall with a sledgehammer. McCurdy again had his nitroglycerin with him.

He placed a charge on the bank vault. It blew the vault door flying through the bank destroying everything in its path. It did not open the safe inside the vault. Blowing up a vault and a safe is a pretty loud undertaking. It could be heard all over town. McCurdy's lookout on the front steps of the bank ran off into the night.

McCurdy and one other man continued to work on the safe. They placed another nitro charge, but it didn't go off. They decided to leave before the police arrived. They stole about $150 in coins that they found unsecured in a drawer. Elmer wasn't making the money he had imagined.

Elmer decided to lay low while he planned his next get-rich scheme. He went to a friend's ranch near Bartlesville, Oklahoma. He boozed it up for a few weeks while living in an outbuilding on the ranch. Then he planned another train robbery. It would be his last.

On October 4, 1911, in an extreme case of bumbling, Elmer and two friends stopped a Missouri-Kansas-Texas Railway train. They heard that it was carrying $400,000 in cash that was to be given to the Osage Nation. They stopped the wrong train. It was an ordinary passenger train.

Elmer and his accomplices stole what they could, but they got very little. Reportedly, they stole a paltry $46, and that was from the mail clerk. They also stole a watch, a coat, and a revolver. None of them were worth very much. The best part of the haul for the alcoholic McCurdy was two large containers of whiskey.

That was it. They expected $400,000. They got $46. Elmer went back to his friend's ranch with the whiskey. He didn't know it, but the authorities were looking for him. They knew who he was and where he was.

On October 7, three sheriffs using bloodhounds tracked McCurdy to where he was staying on the ranch. They ordered him to come out. He began shooting. They returned fire. The battle continued for about an hour.

Eventually the sheriffs realized that McCurdy was no longer

shooting back. They cautiously investigated. McCurdy was dead. He had been struck in the chest by a bullet while he was hiding on the floor. Whether it was an exceptionally bad shot by one of the sheriffs or a ricochet, we will never know. All we know is that Elmer's string of bad luck continued to the very end. He was shot, not when he was actively battling with the sheriffs, but when he was hiding from them.

This concludes the story of Elmer McCurdy's sad life. His story and his bad luck continued on long after his death.

Elmer's body was taken to the Johnson Funeral Home in Pawhuska, Oklahoma. No one claimed it. Joseph Johnson decided to embalm the body and dress it in a black suit. Still no one claimed the body. Johnson refused to bury him without payment. He stored the body in his funeral parlor. And one day, he got an idea how to make some money.

Elmer In His Coffin

He stripped the suit off of Elmer and dressed him in work clothes. He put a rifle in his hands, and stood Elmer in a corner of his funeral home. For a nickel, he would let you see him.

This is where Elmer got the nickname "The Bandit Who Wouldn't Give Up." Johnson gave it to him to stir up business. He also gave him these monikers: The Mystery Man of Many Aliases; The Oklahoma Outlaw; and the Embalmed Bandit."

Elmer gained a little notoriety and fame. Johnson refused a couple of offers to sell. Too bad. It looks like Elmer's bad luck was rubbing off on him.

In October 1916, Johnson was contacted by a man who claimed to be the brother of Elmer. The man had already contacted the sheriff and a local lawyer for their advice and help. Johnson reluctantly agreed to meet him the next day at the funeral parlor.

The next day, that man, who called himself Aver, arrived with another man who also claimed to be a brother. This brother was named Wayne. They took the body and hopped a train to California to bury Elmer.

Well, that's the story they gave to Johnson. In truth, they went to Arkansas City, Kansas. The two men were not Elmer's brothers. They were James and Charles Patterson. They owned a traveling carnival, the Great Patterson Carnival Show. They displayed him for six years. Then they sold him and the rest of their carnival to Louis Sonney who displayed him in his wax Museum of Crime.

Things started getting pretty bad for Elmer after that. He was part of a traveling sideshow following a coast-to-coast footrace called the Trans-American Footrace in 1928. In 1933, he was displayed in theater lobbies to promote an anti-drug movie called Narcotic.

Where he went after that is a mystery until 1949. He was placed in storage that year and remained there until 1964 where he appeared in another film, She Freak. In 1968, believe it or not, poor Elmer was displayed at a show at Mount Rushmore.

Bad Luck Elmer was damaged there. His fingers and toes were blown off. The tips of his ears too. What caused such destruction? The wind. Elmer wasn't in good shape after all those years of exhibition. He was sold to Ed Liersch, owner of an amusement park called The Pike in Long Beach, California. Elmer was about to have the one and only stroke of good luck that he ever had in his life or the decades following.

In 1976, a prop man moved a mannequin out of the way for a scene for the hit show The Six Million Dollar Man. It was Elmer. Depending on which story you prefer, either his arm or his finger broke off.

That started an investigation. It took a while, but they identified him. Curiously, they found the biggest clues in Elmer's mouth. In there, they found a 1924 penny (which dated him as older than that) and a ticket stub to Louis Sonney's Museum of

Crime. They contacted the present-day owners who told them it was, indeed, Elmer.

On April 22, 1977, Elmer was buried in Summit View Cemetery in Guthrie, Oklahoma. He now rests eternally in the Boot Hill section under two solid feet of concrete to ensure that his sleep will never be disturbed.

Some say Elmer's last words were "You'll never take me alive." That's probably a tall tale, but it is quite appropriate. Elmer had an amazing journey after his death. It might have been humiliating and disrespectful, but it was, nonetheless, amazing.

Poor Elmer.

THE TEXAS SPACESHIP OF 1897

Throughout recorded history, there have been many documented UFO incidents. Over 3,000 years ago, the Egyptians reported seeing fiery discs in the sky. There could have been sightings before that time. We'll never know. But there sure are plenty of them since that time. An interesting one happened in 1561 in Nuremberg, Germany. The residents reported seeing a battle in the air followed by a loud crash outside of the city. They said they saw hundreds of objects in the sky.

In more recent times, we have a lot of examples. Pilots began reporting sightings shortly after air travel began. The Roswell incident in 1947 of a crashed alien ship is probably the most famous incident of the last century. The US Navy released a report of their ships being followed for two weeks in 2004 by a "Tic Tac" that easily outperformed their jets. They saw it well enough to describe it as being 45 feet long. During World War II, both Allied and Axis fliers reported seeing strange unexplained things on or near their planes. They were called foo fighters. The Allies thought they were something being developed by the Germans. The Germans probably blamed the Allies.

And of course, there are hundreds and hundreds of less famous sightings of aliens, ships, lights, unexplained phenomena, etc.

But before all of that, we have the story of the alien that crash-landed in Aurora, Texas, on April 17, 1897. According to newspaper accounts, an Army officer from a local post said the pilot was "not of this world." He was buried in the Aurora Cemetery, and many strange things happened after that.

Mary Evans lived in Aurora at that time of the crash. She gave an interview in 1973 in which she said "That crash certainly caused a lot of excitement. Many people were frightened. They didn't know what to expect."

Charlie Stephens was another eyewitness. He was ten at the time of the crash. He said he saw the UFO flying towards Aurora with smoke coming out of it. He wanted to go see it, but his father made him stay on the farm. The next day, his father went to town and saw the crashed ship.

A Windmill Demolishes It.

Aurora, Wise Co., Tex.,April 17.—(To The News.)—About 6 o'clock this morning the early risers of Aurora were astonished at the sudden appearance of the airship which has been sailing through the country.

It was traveling due north, and much nearer the earth than ever before. Evidently some of the machinery was out of order, for it was making a speed of only ten or twelve miles an hour and gradually settling toward the earth. It sailed directly over the public square, and when it reached the north part of town collided with the tower of Judge Proctor's windmill and went to pieces with a terrific explosion, scattering debris over several acres of ground, wrecking the windmill and water tank and destroying the Judge's flower garden.

The pilot of the ship is supposed to have been the only one on board, and while his remains are badly disfigured, enough of the original has been picked up to show that he was not an inhabitant of this world.

Mr. T. J. Weems, the United States signal service officer at this place and an authority on astronomy, gives it as his opinion that he was a native of the planet Mars.

Papers found on his person—evidently the record of his travels—are written in some unknown hieroglyphics, and can not be deciphered.

The ship was too badly wrecked to form any conclusion as to its construction or motive power. It was built of an unknown metal, resembling somewhat a mixture of aluminum and silver, and it must have weighed several tons.

The town is full of people to-day who are viewing the wreck and gathering specimens of the strange metal from the debris. The pilot's funeral will take place at noon to-morrow.   S. E. HAYDON.

Texas Historical Marker at the Aurora, Texas, cemetery

As the story goes, on April 17, 1897, a UFO crashed into a windmill owned by Judge J. S. Proctor. The pilot did not survive, and the townspeople promptly buried him in the Aurora town cemetery. Today, there is a permanent Texas Historical Commission marker in the cemetery about the incident.

The wreckage of the craft wasn't moved but a few feet. The craft hit a windmill which had a well beneath it. The townspeople threw everything down the well and sealed it up. The Dallas Morning News printed the story on April 19, 1897.

Eventually, Judge Proctor sold the property to Brawley Oates. Mr. Oates wanted to reopen the well. He reported a horrible case of arthritis. He blamed it on the water in the well. He had gone down there and fished out all of the metal pieces that he could find.

Mr. Oates decided not to use the well. He sealed it up, put a concrete slab on top of it, and put a building on top of the slab.

The alien's grave has never been dug up, but there have been plenty of attempts. The town does not allow any digging, but it has allowed ground radar, but that was inconclusive.

The well is a different story. Tim Oates, grandson of Brawley Oates, allowed the well to be explored. They didn't find any metal, but they knew that Brawley had tried to remove all of it years ago. They took samples of the water. All they found was an unexplained high level of aluminum.

And that is it for the evidence. If there was a spaceship, Brawley Oates removed it from the well years ago. If there is an alien in the cemetery, the town won't let anyone dig to find out for sure.

The story is a bit bigger than just this one incident. There were reports worldwide during the 1880s and 1890s of aliens and UFOs. In America, there were quite a few sightings in 1896 and 1897.

Some people reported seeing strange lights. Others said they saw ships and crew members. Colonel H. G. Shaw of Stockton, California stated that he came upon a UFO in a field in 1896. Two aliens approached him and tried to force him to enter their craft, but he was too strong for them, and they flew away without him. There were various other reports. In general, the first sightings were on the West Coast, and later ones were further and further east. This led to speculation that the sightings were of hot air balloons. We'll never know because no one ever captured any balloons, aircraft, or aliens.

Although, there are plenty of other UFO stories, sightings and reports from the Wild West, none of them have as many eyewitnesses as the Aurora, Texas, UFO Incident.

THE MARFA LIGHTS

Marfa, Texas, is a very small town in West Texas near Big Bend National Park. As of 2010, there were 1,981 residents. Originally, Marfa was simply a water stop for passing trains. Steam trains must have a ready supply of water. Towns like Marfa often had a water tower as their first permanent building.

A train would pull up. From the water tower would come a spigot arm. Once it was positioned over the proper spot on the tender, the boiler man would put a cord and water would flow into the tender.

This gave rise to the term "jerkwater town." Trains stopped there, but not for passengers or freight. They stopped so they could jerk the cord and water their train. Marfa was the epitome of the term.

The Marfa Lights caught the public eye around 1950, but they were known long before. On a clear night, they move about in different shapes and patterns. They merge and split, dip and zoom, blink out and reappear. They are often described as balls of light. Sometimes, they are lightly colored.

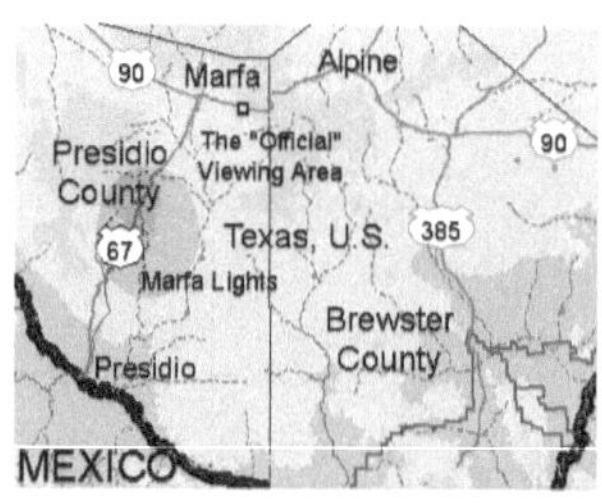

*Map of the Marfa area showing where the Marfa
Lights appear and the best observation area.*

Research has been done in recent decades. One explanation is "atmospheric" reflections of automobile headlights from a nearby highway and/or campfires. In other words, the light from the cars or the campfires bounces off the clouds and then back to earth. Another is a bending of light due to the sometimes extreme temperature fluctuations (40 or more degrees) that sometimes happen in the area.

Those are two dominant theories, but both of them depend on light coming from man-made sources. The area around Marfa was basically uninhabited when the first documented reports came in.

The first reported sighting was by Robert Reed Ellison in 1883. He is sometimes identified as Robert Ellison or Robert Reed. He was working his cattle by himself. He was moving them through the nearby Paisano Pass towards what would become Marfa. There were no sightings before that time, but then again, there were practically no people in the area.

Legend says that Ellison shared his story with his fellow cowboys, and they told him that local Indians were well acquainted with the lights.

The second sighting came shortly after that. In 1885, settlers Joseph and Anne Humphreys, aka Sally Humphreys, reported seeing "dancing lights" in the distance.

The city of Marfa has an official Marfa Lights Viewing Center. The lights do not always appear, but when they do, they are spectacular.

More than a few groups have done studies in the area. Some were quite scientific. Generally, they report that the lights are due to car lights and the occasional campfire. One oddity is that the scientific studies mainly report that the lights appear in predictable patterns.

This doesn't agree with what the casual eyewitness reports. Most of them say the lights dance in irregular patterns, whereas the researchers say the lights move in straight lines.

Perhaps the researchers are somehow altering the situation with their equipment, radios, lights, etc. For instance, researchers always say they can reproduce the lights by driving cars down a nearby highway. Maybe they can. But they can't tell us why the very next day, when the researchers are gone, car lights from that very same highway don't necessarily produce any Marfa Lights.

It's a mystery that has its roots much earlier than cars and highways. Settlers and cowboys saw the lights. The Indians that came before them saw the lights. Perhaps the lights were always there. Perhaps the lights will always be there in the future – with or without automobile lights.

THE PLATTE RIVER SHIP OF DEATH

One of the lesser known legends of the Old West is the Platte River Ship of Death. The earliest documented report was in 1862. Some say the ship appears about every quarter of a century.

This legend has all the trappings of a movie of the week or maybe a Twilight Zone episode. It has ghosts, a haunted ship, a thick fog, and death. There is always death. The kicker is that the person who sees the ship always knows the person who will die.

In the fall of 1862, a trapper named Leon Webber (possibly Weber) reported seeing a deep icy fog roll in on the Platte River, but it wasn't a normal fog. This fog was concentrated in one place. That's strange enough, but there is more. Oh, boy, is there more.

Mr. Webber says a ship came out of the fog. It was a large ship with sails. As it came past him, he clearly saw the crew on the deck standing in front of something. They stood there silently, looking down at the deck. They were covered in frost. As the ship passed him, the crew members stepped aside. There was a young woman lying on the deck. She was dead. To Mr. Webber's horror, he recognized the woman as his fiancee.

At the moment he saw the ship, his fiancee was alive and well back in town. She was dead by nightfall. Mr. Webber heard the sad news when he returned from trapping several days later.

That is the basic story of everyone who sees the Platte River Ship of Death. The dead person is always well known to the person who sees the ship. There is always a strange fog, a sailing ship, and a crew on deck standing in front of the dead person.

Captain Gene Wilson reported seeing the ship in 1887. This time, it was his wife that was lying on the deck. He reported that he was herding cattle near the river when his dog started barking and his horse tried to run back into the trees. The crew was covered in frost as usual. This time, one of the crew ordered the others to lower a piece of canvas to the deck. When it was on the deck, the canvas unfolded and revealed his wife. She was dead by the time he got back to town. Their house had burned down. She lost her life trying to save it.

Another sighting was in 1903. Victor Heibe was trimming bushes and doing yard work on his property bordering the Platte River. First thing was the unusual fog. Then the sailing ship appeared out of the mist. Most other accounts described the ship as being coated with frost. Mr. Heibe, however, reported more than frost. He said the ship was covered in ice.

An unusual aspect of this incident is that he clearly heard voices. One voice angrily proclaimed his innocence. Several others were heard murmuring that they were only doing their duty.

As it slowly passed by, the crew stepped aside and revealed a ghastly sight. It was a good friend of his, hanging from a rope. Once again, the ship foretold the future. His friend did not make it to morning. He died that same day. His friend was a criminal who had previously escaped from jail. He was caught and hanged before nightfall.

If you want to try your luck at spotting the Ship of Death, most sightings are between the Wyoming towns of Torrington and Alcova. Several very recent sightings have been near Casper.

All sightings occur in the late fall. Photographs never develop properly. They are always hazy and foggy showing absolutely nothing.

BIG NOSE GEORGE AND THE GOVERNOR'S SHOES

Big Nose George went by a variety of names. The first name was always George, but the last name was Parrott, Manuse or Warden. Most say his real name was Parrott. Some say Manuse. When Big Nose gave an interview in jail, he called himself Warden. So take your pick as to his last name. Besides that, he had two nicknames. He was Big Nose George when he was Manuse or Warden. When he used the last name Parrott, he went by Big Beak Parrott.

There is also some confusion as to whether he was George Curry. He was not. George Curry was a member of Butch Cassidy's Wild Bunch. His nicknames were Flat-Nose and occasionally Big Nose. So there is similarity between the names of the two men, but they are definitely not the same person. Big Nose George was dead and buried long before Flat-Nose joined Butch Cassidy.

Big Nose George Parrott

No one knows where or when George was born or where he lived his early life. Our story concerns mostly the last four years of his life. Not much else is known.

Big Nose George Parrott was a small-time crook who should have stayed with stickups and cattle rustling, but he had aspirations of greatness. He successfully robbed a few stagecoaches if the tales can be believed. He did pull off one absolutely brilliant robbery. It was an amazing robbery. It led to his downfall.

George would rob or steal something and then head to the safety of the Big Horn Mountains in northern Wyoming. This area was to become famous as the Hole-in-the-Wall country. The pass leading to it is the actual Hole in the Wall. Once a bad guy got beyond the pass, there was nothing but open land and other outlaws.

He was a minor crook at first. A couple of cows here, a stickup there. Around 1878, he joined a loosely organized gang of outlaws. One of them, Sim Jan, may have been the leader. Big Nose said Jan was the leader in an interview he gave while awaiting trial in 1880. He may have been telling a stretcher to make himself look better in his trial. Big Nose was more likely the leader. Other members were Dutch Charley Burress, Frank

McKinney, Joe Manuse, Frank Tole, Jack Campbell, Tom Reed, and John Wells.

They robbed stagecoaches with some success. They didn't know it, but they were already pushing their luck. The law was starting to focus on them. They should have been smart and cooled their heels for a while. They did the opposite. They didn't lay low. They decided to kick it up a notch and rob trains.

The plan was to loosen a rail near Medicine Bow, Wyoming, and wait for a train to come by and crash. Some say they merely loosened a spike and were waiting in the bushes to pull out the spike with a length of wire. Sounds a bit like the Three Stooges or maybe a Roadrunner cartoon. Why not just take out the spike right then and there? In any case, it was a bad plan. They shouldn't have tried it so near a town. A repair crew wandered by. Some started repairing the track. A couple went forward to warn the approaching train.

The gang members were watching all of this happen from the trees near the track. They had an argument over what to do, but eventually they decided to walk away with empty hands.

The law and the Union Pacific Railroad were not forgiving of the bungling outlaws. The train was carrying the payroll for the railroad. They weren't about to let Big Nose get away without punishment. From that day forward, they were constantly hounded until caught and arrested.

After the aborted train robbery, the whole gang took off for Rattlesnake Canyon near Elk Mountain. They didn't go far enough. The railroad was determined to catch them. They sent Sheriff's Deputy Robert Widdowfield and a Union Pacific railroad detective named Henry Vincent. The gang knew they were being followed. What they did next sealed their fate.

The gang holed up inside Rattlesnake Canyon. They put lookouts on the ridges. One of them spotted the lawmen approaching.

The gang knew they couldn't sneak out of the canyon. The only way out was the way they came in, and that path was blocked by Widdowfield and Vincent.

They put out their campfires and hid in the nearby brush. The officers approached. Widdowfield knelt and stirred the embers of the fire. They were still hot, and Widdowfield knew that meant they were near. He called to Vincent, and that started the attack from the gang. Widdowfield went down first, shot in the face.

Vincent fared only a little better. He fought his way out of the campsite, but they killed him before he left the canyon.

The gang hid the bodies and stole their weapons. One outlaw's horse had been injured in the attack; so they took one of the lawmen's. They scattered the rest of the horses.

And at that, they took off again. This time, they knew they would be chased. They ran hard and kept to the shadows. The Union Pacific was furious when it found out about the murders. They offered $10,000 for the arrest of the murderers. Soon after, they upped the reward to $20,000. The railroad wanted them caught, and they wanted them caught right now.

The gang wasn't caught. At least, not yet. They stayed out of sight for the rest of 1878, but early the next year, they staged their greatest robbery.

In early 1879, Big Nose George, Dutch Charley, and two other gang members were in Milestown (Miles City), Montana. They learned that a businessman was sending money back East. The man, Morris Cahn, felt safe. He would be traveling with a detachment of troops that were on their way to pick up a payroll.

When they left town, Cahn was accompanied by 15 soldiers, two officers, the payroll wagon, and an ambulance. Big Nose and his three friends captured all of them. It was a thing of beauty.

Near Terry, Montana is a deep coulee, a type of ravine created by water runoff. This coulee is now known as Cahn's Coulee because of what happened that day.

Whether it happened to avoid eating each other's dust or whether the detachment had trouble, we will never know, but they arrived at Cahn's Coulee spread out with much too much distance between them.

They entered the coulee in three groups. First in were the lead soldiers. Then the ambulance entered, along with Cahn and the two officers. Finally the rear guard entered the coulee.

The coulee was deep and winding. They couldn't see much except what was directly in front of them. Big Nose George and his three friends waited behind a bend in the coulee. Without a shot, they captured the first group of soldiers, then the second group with Cahn, and finally the trailing soldiers. Not a shot fired. If you are a fan of outlaws, this one was a masterpiece.

Cahn, of course, was robbed. Cahn said he carried $14,000 with him. The gang said it was just $3,600. The payroll wagon was empty. They had not yet picked up the Army money.

With the soldiers disarmed and their horses driven away, the outlaws had an easy time riding away. Two of them rode off by themselves never to be heard of again.

The other two, Big Nose George and Dutch Charley foolishly went back to Milestown. Big Nose and Charley got drunk and started bragging about killing lawmen. Before long, someone alerted the law.

Two deputies, Lem Wilson and Fred Schmalsle bravely confronted and arrested them. Once behind bars, the deputies inquired as to who they had killed. Perhaps it wouldn't have mattered in the long run, but the outlaws willingly spilled their guts. The whole story came out.

Wilson and Schmalsle were stunned. They captured the men that the Union Pacific and the law had been after without success for two years. And they did it without gunfire. They just walked into the bar and arrested two very drunk and very stupid outlaws.

Another account says that Big Nose was alone in that bar because Dutch Charley had been previously captured. In any event, both outlaws were caught and then sent by separate trains from Montana to Wyoming.

Dutch Charley's train was commandeered by a lynching party when it stopped in Carbon, Wyoming, for water. They dragged Charley off the train, and hung a noose over a telegraph pole. They put Charley on top of a barrel, and asked him if he had any last words.

Out of the crowd stepped the widow of Deputy Widdowfield. She said, "No, the SOB has nothing to say," and she kicked the barrel out from under him. That was the end of Dutch Charley.

The town refused to bury him in their cemetery. Deputy Widdowfield was buried there. Dutch Charley was buried in an unmarked grave somewhere outside of town.

Big Nose George almost suffered the same fate.

Carbon County Sheriff James Rankin traveled to Montana and brought Big Nose back to Wyoming to stand trial. That train was stopped by the same mob that lynched Dutch Charley.

They dragged Big Nose off the train. The mob threw a rope over a telegraph pole. Big Nose started crying and begging for his life. He pleaded with them and promised to tell all he knew about his past crimes. The mob relented. They allowed Sheriff Rankin to continue the trip to Rawlins for the trial.

He was arraigned in September 1880, and the trial began in November. He was quickly sentenced to hang. The date chosen was April 2, 1881.

Well, Big Nose wasn't ready to accept his fate. He acquired a pocketknife in prison. With it, he scraped at the pins holding his leg shackles locked. Little by little, he scraped until he freed himself.

On March 22, less than two weeks before his scheduled hanging, he slipped out of his shackles and hid himself in a washroom. Sheriff Rankin entered the cell area, and Big Nose jumped him. He struck him in the head with the shackles. Rankin went down with blood streaming in his eyes, but he continued fighting. He called out for help.

Rankin was lucky he was married. His wife, Rosa, was the only one who heard his screams. She came running with a revolver. She slammed the main cell door, trapping Big Nose for good. Then she fired off a shot, and citizens came running to her aid.

News of the attempted escape soon made its way through town. The citizens were incensed. They stormed the jail. They had little trouble overpowering the seriously injured Sheriff Rankin. Big Nose was dragged outside.

What followed was an unbelievably vicious hanging.

Big Nose was pleading with them. He got no sympathy. The town had had enough. A crowd of over 200 people called for his hanging. They threw a rope over a telegraph pole on Front Street and hauled him up on a barrel. They kicked the barrel out from under him. "Dance, you bastard," they cried.

And the rope broke.

Big Nose gasped for air. He begged to be shot. Some say they hung him a second time and failed a second time.

For the final attempt, they weighed him down with the shackles he had removed. Then they had him climb a high ladder. His hands for some reason were not bound behind his back. They were free.

When they kicked the ladder out from under him, Big Nose held on with his hands. The shackles were heavy and were pulling him down. He held on. And on. And on. Then as his arms tired, the noose tightened around his throat, and he slowly strangled to death.

The slow agonizing hanging had another dreadful effect. His ears were completely worn off. This shows up in the death mask that was later made of his face. The rope took his ears when the mob took his life.

Big Nose George was dead. His story, however, was far from over.

There is a theory that what happened next was the result of revenge. Do you remember the train robbery that never happened? The one where they loosened a rail, but a train crew repaired it before an accident happened? Well, that train wasn't derailed or robbed, but it was delayed.

Now a few years after that train non-robbery, Dr. Thomas Maghee and Dr. John Eugene Osborne were presented with the body of Big Nose George. Dr. Maghee wanted to study the brain. His interest was science. If he discovered a difference in the brain of an outlaw perhaps it would help him find a cure for his wife who had suffered a severe brain injury.

Dr. Osborne wanted – well, he wanted revenge. Legend says he was on that delayed train and it made him miss an important party. Osborne had political ambitions, and the delay of the train also delayed his plans. Now that Osborne had the body of the man responsible, he was ready and willing to slice and dice. And that is exactly what he did.

He skinned Big Nose. He made a doctor's bag, a coin purse, and a pair of shoes from the skin. Dr. Maghee sawed off the top of Big Nose's head and scooped out the brain. For some reason, they gave top of the skull to a local teenage girl named Lillian Heath who eventually became a doctor herself. She kept the skull all of her life. She put it to several ordinary uses much like you would use a small bowl or dish. Among other things, she used it as a pen holder, a doorstop, and an ashtray.

The doctors kept the rest of the body in a barrel. Eventually, they buried it behind Dr. Maghee's office where it remained until it was dug up by a construction crew in 1950.

Dr. Osborne loved his shoes. He really did use Big Nose's skin for the shoes, but not the whole shoe. He used the skin for the front half of the shoe, but not the part with the tongue and laces. The rest of the shoe was made from the actual shoes that Big Nose was wearing when he was hung.

He wore those shoes at every special occasion. He wore them as a doctor. He wore them when he rose to become the chairman of a bank. He wore them to parties where he hobnobbed with high society as one of the richest men in Wyoming.

And he wore them when he was inaugurated third governor of the State of Wyoming.

Big Nose George was never fully put to rest. The barrel of bones was reburied, but that's it. The top of the skull was given to the Union Pacific Museum in Council Bluffs, Iowa, and they aren't giving it back. The shoes are now in the Rawlins, Wyoming, museum, along with a death mask of Big Nose's face, and other gruesome mementos.

THE INTERTWINED LIVES OF MASS MURDERERS CHARLES KENNEDY AND CLAY ALLISON

When Serial Killers Meet

The best thing you can say about Charles Kennedy is he wasn't a cannibal. Oh, sure, he'd kill you, but he wouldn't eat you.

Good ol' Mr. Kennedy had a fine game plan. He owned the only piece of civilization near the Palo Flechado Pass in New Mexico close to the small town of Elizabethtown. Travelers would stop in on their way to or from Taos, have dinner, and then Mr. Kennedy would kill and rob them.

Charley was a big man. He had little trouble overpowering his victims. He simply caught them unawares, and it was over quickly. Since his prey were travelers, their disappearance didn't raise any alarms.

Reportedly, he killed 14 people. He was only caught when he turned on his family.

As the story was told by his wife, Charley, his young son, and a traveler were having the evening meal. The traveler innocently asked if there were any Indians in the area. For whatever reason, Charley's son responded by saying "Can't you smell the one Papa put under the floor?"

Charley flew into a deadly rage. He shot the man dead. He killed his son by bashing his head on the stones of the fireplace. Both bodies were thrown into his cellar. He beat up his wife and locked her in the bedroom. Then he got drunk. Really drunk.

His wife waited until he passed out. Then she escaped and ran to Elizabethtown. The first place she found was a saloon. She staggered in and collapsed in a heap. When she recovered, she told the men all about Charley and his murderous ways. One of the men in the bar that night was Clay Allison, a gunman of violent temper. He led a group of men to Charley's house that night.

Charley was still drunk as a skunk. They tied him up and then searched the house. They found bodies, bones, and skeletons. The bodies were of his son and the traveler. The bones were of some anonymous victim. They were being consumed by the fire. The skeletons were unfortunates that Charley was too lazy to burn or bury.

Clay Allison had little use or respect for the law as you will see a little later in this story, but the group persuaded him to take Charley to the authorities. Charley was arraigned. A witness testified that he saw Charley murder one of the travelers. Charley was ordered to be held without bail until trial.

Rumors started moving around town that Charley was going to buy his freedom with a crooked judge. My, oh, my, that did not sit well with the town. They weren't going to let that happen. Something had to be done, and it had to be done quickly. They stormed the jail in a collective rage. They battered down the front door. They broke the lock on the cell. They dragged Charley into the street.

And then they solved the problem by dragging Charley Kennedy behind a horse until he was dead.

No one was arrested. The incident was barely investigated. Miserable, bloodthirsty Charley had no friends to stand up for him. The town buried him, but not in their cemetery. He's out there somewhere in the countryside in an unmarked grave.

Now you might think that his death would stop the killing. Nope. As it turns out, the townspeople that killed him were pretty bad themselves. The leader was Clay Allison, and he was a deadly killer. He called himself a vigilante and a shootist, but murdering bully is probably a better term.

Allison was a leader in the Colfax Country War in which almost 200 people died. He lynched a local policeman. He thought the policeman worked as a killer for the other side; so he killed him first.

He may have been as maniacal a killer as Charles Kennedy, but he had more than his share of offbeat stories. In several of them during the Civil War, he screamed and fought with his officers when they withdrew from battle or stopped pursuit. Eventually, his superiors had enough of Charley. Despite needing every able-bodied man, they forced him out of the Army. On his discharge papers it read: "Emotional or physical excitement produces paroxysmal of a mixed character, partly epileptic and partly maniacal."

Another story has Allison and a neighbor jumping into a new grave with Bowie knives. The loser would be buried in the grave after the winner crawled out. There is no evidence that this fight actually took place, but it is just one of many stories. Whether true or not, it is accurate as to his callous and violent tendencies.

Part of the Charles Kennedy story concerns what happened to his body after he was killed and before he was buried. Some say that Clay Allison cut off Kennedy's head and carried it almost 30 miles to Cimarron where it was displayed on a stake in front of what became the St. James Hotel. Whether this story is true is also subject to dispute. No reason is given as to why Allison would do such a thing. Why not display him in Elizabethtown?

What make such a trip to a town that neither Allison or Kennedy had any real connection? Who knows? Take your own guess.

One story that we know is true is the big shootout that he had with Wyatt Earp. Well, it wasn't really a shootout. It was more like a showdown. Well, maybe not a showdown either. One version of the story is that Allison and his pals ran roughshod over Dodge City while Earp and Bat Masterson fled the town. Another version (this one by Earp) is that Allison was convinced to leave town by Wyatt and his deputies. A third version seems to be the most likely since it was given by Pinkerton detective Charles Siringo. In this version, Allison was convinced to leave town by a couple of cowboys and a saloon owner. Siringo said if Earp and Allison did meet, it was only for a moment.

There are plenty of authentic accounts of Allison's bloody ways. He was a born killer with many deaths to his credit. Even ordinary situations could explode into fantastic fights. He once yanked out a dentist's tooth and was going in for another when the frightened dentist's screams brought town members to his rescue. He once forced a sheriff to drink until the poor man fell over in a stupor.

Clay Allison's tombstone in Pecos, Texas

His eventual death was not the result of a gunfight or his bad temper. It was, however, another odd occurrence in his life. One day he was carrying supplies to his new ranch by wagon. A sack of grain started to slip off. Allison reached for it and fell off the wagon. The wheels rolled over his neck, instantly killing him.

We'll conclude this chapter with one final story about Clay Allison.

Besides being a coldhearted murderer, Allison was also more than a bit strange. He was known to occasionally ride through town wearing only his gun belt. After killing one man in a saloon, he reportedly pranced around the bar naked with a red ribbon on his penis.

Hopefully, it was a big ribbon or a dark saloon.

THE LITTLEST SKYSCRAPER IN THE WORLD

The Wichita Falls Practical Joke
Heard 'Round the World

As the days of the cowboy were winding down, the days of the oil boom were, well, booming. In Texas and Oklahoma, they were finding oil all over. Towns sprang up overnight. Fortunes were made on a handshake. Money flowed freely.

Wichita Falls, Texas, was smack in the middle of it. A huge oil reservoir was found under the nearby town of Burkburnett in 1912. In six years, 20,000 people flooded into the area. New towns were started. Sleepy country towns soared in population.

Wichita Falls, the largest town in the area, became home to the oilmen, and it grew quickly. The town constantly needed more offices, more stores, more homes. It was build, build, build during the boom.

One of the town's leading citizens at the time was J. D. McMahon. All the big money knew J. D. He owned a construction firm that specialized in oil rigs. He was a petroleum landman and a structural engineer. He did everything from ne-gotiating contracts to buying mineral rights to inspecting rigs and structures for safety. The big money in town loved him.

The other oilmen hired J. D. or his firm on a regular basis. He was known to be friendly, accommodating, and knowledgeable. Everybody liked him.

The World's Littlest Skyscraper, the
Newby-McMahon Building

J. D. rented space in the Newby Building which was built in 1906, just six years before the discovery of oil. There wasn't much choice. Wichita Falls couldn't build fast enough to keep up with the demand for offices, warehouses, and the like.

Mr. Newby occupied one of the two offices in the two-story building. J. D. and six other tenants shared the other office. J. D. wanted more room. He had a plan.

And what a plan it was.

This author believes that J. D. started out with the honest intentions of helping the town. Somewhere, somehow, he took a wrong turn. J. D. got the idea of playing an elaborate practical joke on the town. It cost him his firm and his reputation, but his joke will be remembered forever.

In 1919, J. D. McMahon, respected wealthy oilman and leading citizen, announced that he would solve the office space problem. He was going to build a high-rise skyscraper that soared into the air. It would be the jewel of Wichita Falls.

The oilmen rushed to invest their money with their good friend and fellow oilman. J. D. collected a cool $200,000. That's about $3 million in today's money.

They had business meetings to discuss the deal. Then they had a lot of parties to celebrate it. Blueprints were drawn up. Everybody looked them over. Approval was given. Contracts were signed by all parties.

And work began on the glorious Wichita Falls Skyscraper. J. D. used his own construction crew. They were quick and competent. The land was cleared, and work began.

It did not take long before the questions started. Accusations weren't far behind. The building J. D. was constructing was small. Really small. Impossibly small.

J. D. gave them his best innocent smile. He assured them that everything was proceeding on time and according to specifications. His crew continued with the construction of the tiny structure.

The town was incensed. They brought J. D. to court. They sued him. They brought the evidence. They had the contracts, the plans, and the blueprints. And J. D. gave them his best innocent smile.

The judge looked at the evidence. The investors' complaint was that they signed a contract for a skyscraper 480 feet high, 100 feet wide and 160 feet long. Instead, J. D. built a tiny building only 40 feet high and definitely not 100 feet wide or 160 feet long.

To the dismay of the investors, the judge ruled in favor of J. D. The judge said the contract was fully carried out, and the building was exactly what was called for in the contract.

They couldn't believe it. They had the contract. They had the blueprints. Everything was laid out in those blueprints, and every investor had read and approved those blueprints.

The judge explained his decision. According to the blueprints, the building specifications were in inches, not feet. J. D. built them a building that was 480 inches (40 feet) high. Since no one could testify that they heard J. D. ever say the building would be 480 feet high, the judge couldn't rule fraud. The contract had been fulfilled, and the investors lost their case.

J. D. McMahon, oilman and con artist, quickly left town never to return. He took with him the bulk of the investors $200,000.

That's the story that is told by almost every historian, but it has giant holes that can't be explained. The biggest one is the judge's decision, of course. It was dead wrong.

J. D. built his four-story white elephant on the lot next to the Newby Building. According to the story above, he said he was building an annex to it. The trouble with that is that J. D. didn't own that land. Neither did Mr. Newby. That section of land was owned by Mabel Jones, the niece of Mr. Newby. She lived in Oklahoma. She was not aware that anyone was building on her property.

There is no doubt as to the ownership of the land. It was clearly recognized as her land during the time of the trial. No one ever disputed it.

Which brings us to the judge's decision. J. D. may have built according to specifications, but he did not deliver that building to the investors. They could not take ownership. It wasn't their land, and therefore, it wasn't their building. Any judge would have ruled that the contract was not fulfilled and/or that J. D. committed fraud.

If that story isn't true, then perhaps, the alternate one is true. Perhaps. If it is, then my thoughts of J. D. playing an elaborate joke are probably also true.

It is very difficult to find any other version of the events, except the one with the trial and judge's decision. Wichita Falls does have a one-page, unsigned, undated account of an alternate version of events that seems a lot more likely.

According to the alternate version, J. D. did raise $200,000 from investors, but he wasn't sneaky about the size of the building. It was to be a state-of-the-art building with plenty of offices, stores, and apartments.

That isn't to say that J. D. wasn't intending to flim-flam the town. He told them how high it would be, but he didn't let them know where it would be. That happens at times. You have to find a suitable section and negotiate with the owners before you can buy it.

He did build the four-story building on the lot owned by Ms. Jones right next to the Newby building. It is standing there today. He didn't tell anybody he was building it, and it was such a small building that nobody took notice of it. Mr. Newby probably thought Ms. Jones, his niece, was constructing it. The niece lived in Oklahoma. She had no idea that it was being built. Nobody else in town had any interest in it.

J. D. never started construction on the high-rise building. He skipped town with the money shortly after the tiny building, the Littlest Skyscraper, was completed.

The other renters in the Newby building shared one telephone because they all worked in the same office. They reported taking calls for months asking about the wonderful skyscraper that J. D. was building. They didn't know what to tell them.

One of those calls was answered by a tenant with construction experience. He asked for the specifications and address of the building. The caller said it was 40-stories high, and the address was 701 La Salle. It was the alley behind the Newby building.

The tenant knew Wichita Falls didn't have a 40-story building. He certainly knew there wasn't one in the tiny two-block alley called La Salle Street. But he went and checked anyway.

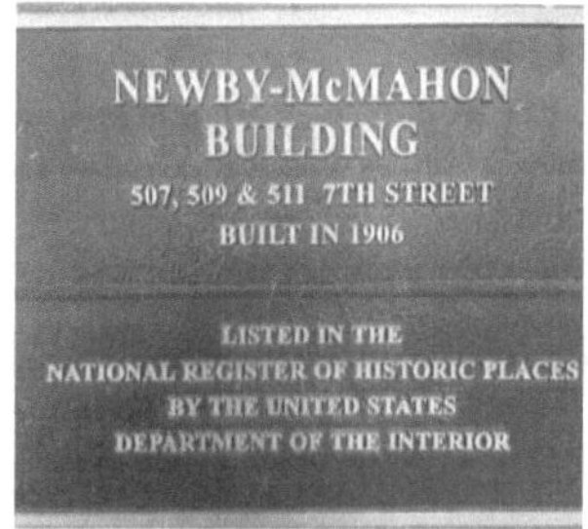

Plaque attached to the Newby-McMahon building

701 La Salle was the address of the tiny building someone had built next to the Newby Building. The tenant, since he had construction experience, measured the building as to height, width, and length. He burst out laughing.

He found J. D.'s building. It was the exact size he said it would be, except that the measurements were in inches instead of feet.

The Littlest Skyscraper stands proudly (sort of) today in Wichita Falls as a tourist attraction. It is a nondescript building that has spent most of its life unoccupied. It is still tiny, of course.

MA BENDER AND HER BLOODY FAMILY

*A Family (Maybe) of Cold-
Blooded Killers (Definitely)*

Ma Bender was the leader of a pack of vicious serial killers. History knows them as the Bloody Benders, and boy, oh, boy, did they live up to their name.

They terrorized travelers and the residents of Labette County, Kansas, for two years. From 1871 to 1873, at least 11 and up to 20 or more people went missing. Many of them were later found buried on the grounds of the Bender homestead.

The Benders first came to Labette County when it was opened to homesteaders. The government had moved the Osage Indians to the Indian Territory in what was to become Oklahoma. Almost everyone in Labette County was a homesteader and/or had just arrived.

*The Bender Family from the 1913 book The
Benders in Kansas by John Towner James*

The Benders fit right in. They arrived in a group of five families. Some have called them spiritualists which are people who believe the spirits of the dead are alive and are willing to communicate and help the living.

The first to arrive were John (sometimes known as William) Bender and his son, John Jr. (sometimes Thomas). They registered 160 acres of land near the Great Osage Trail (Santa Fe Trail) which was the best "road" west at the time, especially if you were pulling a wagon or two. Travelers were always passing by their property.

Their land was undeveloped as was most of the land in the area. The Benders dug a well and built a one-room cabin with windows and peaked roof. At that point, they sent word to Elvira, the mother, and Kate, the daughter. By the time they arrived in late 1871, the two Bender men had added a barn with a corral.

The women divided the house into two sections with a canvas tarp from their wagon. The rear section was the private area for all four Benders. The front served as the kitchen, dining room, general store, and occasional sleeping quarters for visitors. They sold supplies such as gun powder, rifle shot, tobacco, liquor, flour, sugar, and salt. It wasn't pretty or comfortable, but if you were traveling the Great Osage Trail, you didn't have much choice.

The Bender Inn

Elvira and Kate planted a few acres of vegetables and some apple trees. Fresh fruit and vegetables were hard to find on the road west. This made their little rest stop a lot more attractive. Travelers subsisted on what they could carry in their wagons and what fresh game they could kill. Fresh fruits and vegetables were hard to come by on the road.

John Sr. and Elvira were 60 and 55 respectively. Neither spoke English very well. John Sr. was very tall and broad with massive eyebrows, black eyes, and a gruff expression. He came to be known as "old beetle-browed John."

Elvira was known as a mean wicked woman. Neighbors called her a she-devil. She claimed to speak to the dead. She boiled concoctions from roots and plants that she used to cast spells, both good and bad. She was tall, heavy-set and imposing. Those who knew the family said she ran the show. The other Benders did her bidding.

John Jr. and Kate were in their mid-twenties. Both were fairly good looking. John had a strange habit of laughing at nothing. Kate appeared to be the most normal of the four. She spoke English well, and became known in the surrounding community for a variety of activities.

Professor Miss Katie Bender presented herself as a healer and a psychic. She gave seances. She lectured on spiritualism. If that isn't enough, she raised a bit of a stir with her own version of free love. Some say she advocated it. Some say she actively practiced it with both sexes.

One of the strangest viewpoints of hers concerned murder. She was a proponent and said it was justified. Oh, those homesteaders should have taken the hint from that one. But no. She was young, attractive, and well-liked. She lectured often.

That is about all that was known about the Benders by the other homesteaders in the area.

Hang onto your hat while I give you some really strange facts and suppositions about this "family."

They were thought to be from Germany, but only the father definitely was. The son possibly was. The women were not.

John Sr. came from either Germany or the Netherlands. Some say his true name was John Flickinger.

Elvira had several husbands before she became a Bender. Rumor is that she killed a few of them. According to newspapers from their time, she was born Almira Hill Mark and her first husband was Simon Mark.

Kate was rumored to be one of 12 children of the Mark marriage. Her full name was Sarah Eliza Mark. Later she married and took the last name Davis.

John Jr. was probably German. He might have been an immigrant from Europe. Others say he was the son of Elvira from an earlier marriage. In the Bender family bible, his name is listed as John Gebhardt. No other Gebhardts are listed, and no one has ever tracked down that name to prove his identity.

John Sr. was not the father of Kate or John Jr. Elvira was the mother of Kate and possibly of John Jr. Kate and John Jr. probably had different fathers.

The family presented John Jr. and Kate as brother and sister. Some of their neighbors claimed that they were actually man and wife.

When you sum all of that up, you have one really strange family. The father wasn't related to the children. The children may have been brother and sister and also man and wife. The mother left a few dead husbands in her wake.

When the bodies started showing up, the Benders were not suspects. There was no reason. The first bodies did not appear near the Benders homestead.

In May, 1871, a man named Jones was discovered in Drum Creek. His throat was slashed, and his skull was caved in. The nearest claim was also called Drum Creek. The owner was blamed, but with no proof, nothing was done.

Two men were found in February, 1872. They also had their throats cut and heads bashed in. Vigilantes started patrolling. Strangers were arrested and jailed, only to be let go later for lack of evidence. Some were driven from the area.

By 1873, the area was being actively avoided. Lone travelers were warned to stay away. Groups were told to stay armed and on guard. They had found several bodies, but plenty of other people had gone missing. Labette County, Kansas, was in the grip of mysterious serial killers that left no evidence.

If you have watched any mystery shows, you know what happens next. Someone starts snooping around looking for a lost daughter, wife, partner, cousin, etc.

In this case, the first investigator was a private citizen, Dr. William Henry York. He was the friend and neighbor of George Longcor. George left Independence, Kansas, in 1872 with his baby daughter. They never arrived in Iowa.

Dr. York went looking for them. Lo and behold, Dr. York went missing. That was a big mistake for the Benders. Dr. York had two influential and powerful brothers. One was Colonel Ed York of the nearby Kansas military post, Fort Scott. The other was Alexander York, Kansas Senator. The two brothers flexed their political and military muscles and set out to find their brother.

Colonel York combed the countryside with 50 men. Every trail was covered. Every traveler was questioned. Every homestead was visited. On March 28, 1873, Colonel York rode to the Bender homestead. They were questioned, but nothing incriminating was discovered. The Benders said Dr. York had stayed with them but had moved on. They raised the possibility of Indian trouble.

Colonel York returned six days later with an armed guard and a woman witness who accused the Benders of trying to kill her with knives. The Benders denied everything. The woman had no physical proof. The Colonel and his party left again. The men with Colonel York thought the Benders and another family, the Roaches, were guilty. York wanted evidence before taking any action.

It was at this point that several strokes of good luck happened to the Benders. First, there was a meeting with the area citizens about what to do. They decided to get search warrants and search homesteads in a wide area. That took a few days to plan. Second, even though the Benders were the prime suspects, nobody was watching them. Third, when it was reported that the Benders had abandoned their homestead, bad weather kept them from investigating.

On the other hand, they had several hundred local volunteers and Colonel York's men. All of them descended on the Bender homestead. They uncovered everything quickly.

A terrible stench was in the house. It was traced to a trap door under a bed. It led to a small room just large enough for a body or two. It was a temporary hiding place.

The men outside quickly found graves, plenty of graves. Dr. York's body was discovered. They moved the entire house looking for bodies, but none were in the cabin floor. They found most of the bodies in the vegetable garden and the orchard. One body was in the only well that the Benders had. They used that water for cooking, drinking, cleaning.

The actual number of bodies found depends on how you look at it. They didn't find full skeletons for some. The number is at least 11, but it could easily be double that.

Here's what the Benders would do: They would position a guest so his back was to the canvas curtain that divided the cabin. One of the Bender men would strike the traveler with a hammer from behind the curtain. Once dazed or dead, the women would quickly slash the victim's throat while the men were opening the trap door. The body was dumped into the small room below.

When they did it right, the body could be disposed of in under a minute. The searchers discovered bullet holes in the cabin walls and ceiling. Apparently some of the victims put up a struggle.

The Benders did not act fully alone. They sold the victims' belongings to people in the area. Twelve people were arrested and charged with being accessories to their crimes.

The Benders were tracked for a while. The wagon they used was found near Thayer, a small town just 12 miles away. All four boarded the train.

The younger couple, John Jr. and Kate went south to Texas

and then to a lawless area on the Texas/New Mexico border. They were never seen again. There were rumors that John Jr. died of apoplexy, a stroke. Nothing was ever heard of Kate.

The elder Benders were thought to take several trains before arriving in St. Louis where the trail went cold. Despite a $3,000 reward, they were never heard of again.

Well, that's the official story. There are unsubstantiated stories that vigilantes shot or lynched them. One group said they burned Kate alive. Another story says Pa Bender committed suicide.

In 1884, an old man matching Pa Bender's description killed a man with a hammer. He was being held in Montana. Authorities in Kansas sent a deputy. Before he could get there, the suspect cut off his foot trying to escape. He escaped his leg irons, but then promptly bled to death. By the time the deputy got there, the body was badly decomposed and impossible to identify.

In 1889, it appeared that the Bender women were caught in Michigan for larceny. Their true identities were discovered, and they were put on trial for the Bender murders. Both women denied being Benders. It was a very confusing trial. At one point the younger woman claimed the older one was Ma Bender. She said she was not Kate. She was Kate's sister Sara. The older woman said she was not Ma Bender, but the younger one was Kate.

Besides that confusing testimony, there was other testimony supporting both women and almost no real evidence against them. The judge had no choice but to find that they were not the Benders.

After the trial, there weren't any more "sightings" of the Benders. Maybe they got away. Maybe they were hanged or shot by vigilantes. No one knows, and apparently no one ever will.

THE REVENGE OF THE THREE GUARDSMEN

The Long Arm of the Law
Has a Long Memory Too

William Matthew Tilghman Jr. carried a gun all of his life, most of it as a lawman. He was marshal of Dodge City in the early 1880s. He had a hand in the Kansas County Seat Wars. He was a US Marshal in the Oklahoma Territory. He captured Bill Doolin, head of the Doolin Gang and founder of the Wild Bunch.

In 1915, at the age of 61, his life story was made into a movie. He starred in it. He even directed it.

Nine years later, in 1924, he was shot and killed in Cromwell, Oklahoma. His killing, and the resulting backlash, forms the basis of this story.

Marshal Tilghman was one of three US Marshals known as the Three Guardsmen. The other two were Chris Madsen and Heck Thomas. All three worked under US Marshal Evett E. D. Nix.

Marshal Tilghman, 1912

They earned their name because of their relentless pursuit of outlaws. In fact, it was the outlaws that gave them the nickname.

Christen Madsen Rormose took a strange path to becoming an American hero. He was born in Denmark. As a young man, he had several convictions for fraud and forgery. He left Denmark, emigrated to America, and joined the US Army. He dropped his last name. From that point, he went by Chris Madsen.

He rose in rank, fought many battles, and finally retired from the Army in 1891. He promptly hired on as a Deputy Marshal in the Oklahoma Territory.

Madsen killed several members of the Doolin Gang, including Dynamite Dick Clifton, George Red Buck Waightman and Richard Little Dick West.

Henry Andrew "Heck" Thomas

The third member of the Three Guardsmen was Heck Thomas. Of the three, Thomas is the only one who died before the Cromwell, Oklahoma, incident.

Together, the Three Guardsmen were credited with over 300 arrests. They broke up the Wild Bunch/Doolin Gang. Heck Thomas was mentioned by name by Emmett Dalton as the reason why the Dalton Gang chose to commit two simultaneous bank robberies in Coffeyville, Kansas.

The gang reasoned that the Three Guardsmen would eventually catch them; so they planned to retire after one last spectacular double robbery. They were wrong. Only Emmett lived, and he had 23 gunshot wounds. After spending 14 years in jail, Emmett made his living writing his memoirs. He spoke of the Three Guardsmen often.

Marshal Heck Thomas killed Bill Doolin, the leader of the gang. He was originally caught by Marshal Tilghman, but he escaped jail six months later. He was shot and killed on August 24, 1896.

Dynamite Dan Clifton and Little Dick West were killed by a posse led by Marshal Chris Madsen. Marshal Tilghman captured Little Bill Raidler.

These three Marshals became famous for their relentless pursuit and capture of any outlaws foolish enough to enter the Oklahoma or Indian Territories.

After they retired, they went their separate ways, but strange as it may seem, they reunited later on to make films. They relived their glory days as lawmen in those films.

Heck Thomas was elected Chief of Police of Lawton, Oklahoma. He served for seven years. Then in 1908, he made a film with Bill Tilghman. Heck played the Marshal, of course. Quanah Parker, leader of the Comanche Nation, had a small part in it. The bad guys were led by Al Jennings, a real-life train robber turned movie actor.

Heck Thomas was the first of the Three Guardsmen to die. He passed away peacefully in Lawton, Oklahoma in 1912. He was 62.

A few years later, Tilghman, Chris Madsen and their old boss, Evett Nix formed a motion picture company, the Eagle Film Company. They produced "The Passing of the Oklahoma Outlaws." Tilghman, Madsen, and Nix appeared as themselves. Today, only a few minutes of the film still survive.

Bill Tilghman from the movie The Passing of the Oklahoma Outlaws

In 1924, Bill Tilghman was sent to Cromwell, Oklahoma, to investigate corruption. Cromwell was founded the year before by Joe Cromwell, a Muskogee oilman. The town exploded in population. Within weeks of its founding, the town had several thousand residents and a serious problem with lawlessness.

Wiley Lynn was the prohibition agent of the government for Cromwell, but he was corrupt. Lynn was associated with Arnold Killian, a known mobster. Cromwell was as wet as any town could be. Cromwell was mostly saloons, brothels and gambling parlors. They had no effective law.

Tilghman would arrest someone for a prohibition violation, and Lynn would get them out of jail. Tilghman didn't have proof against Lynn, but he knew he was taking bribes to keep the bootleggers out of jail.

Half of the town was behind Tilghman. They wanted Cromwell cleaned up and respectable. Half of the town was behind Lynn. They wanted the saloons, brothels and gambling halls to continue.

On November 1, 1924, it came to a head. Tilghman was in Ma Murphy's Cafe with Deputy Marshal Hugh Sawyer. Lynn pulled up in front with prostitutes Eva Caton and Rose Lutke and an Army Sergeant named Thompson. They poured out of their vehicle, and Lynn drunkenly fired off a shot into the air.

Tilghman came charging out of the cafe. He grabbed Lynn, and they wrestled for the gun. With the help of Sawyer, Tilghman disarmed the drunken Lynn.

Suddenly, Lynn pulled out a second gun and shot Tilghman twice in the chest. Then he fled the scene.

There was a trial, but Lynn was acquitted. One witness fled to Florida. He wrote a letter stating he saw Lynn kill Tilghman, but it wasn't allowed in court. Another witness, Rose Lutke, disappeared and was never seen again. Deputy Sawyer helped disarm Lynn, but he testified that he could not clearly see the incident. Bribery and intimidation kept the witnesses from testifying. Lynn walked free.

The town of Cromwell was corrupt. The criminals behind the brothels, gambling, and booze wanted it that way. They cheered the decision to set Lynn free. It infuriated lawmen.

Almost one month to the day, the entire town of Cromwell was set ablaze. No building was left standing. Everything was destroyed. No one knows who set the fire.

The prevailing theory is that the one remaining living member of the Three Guardsmen, Chris Madsen, and a host of sympathetic friends and marshals, set upon the town.

No one was ever arrested. No one was convicted. No one was indicted. In fact, there was no investigation. Whether Madsen took revenge for the death of his friend, we will never know.

The town of Cromwell never recovered. Most residents moved away. As of the 2000 census, Cromwell had 265 residents. Today, it is a small sleepy town with very little crime.

Many years later, Lynn was killed in a fierce gun battle in Madill, Oklahoma, with Oklahoma Agent Crockett Long, a friend of Marshal Tilghman. By this time, Lynn had pretty much destroyed his life. His wife and children left him. He was arrested for various crimes in various towns. His parents still lived in Madill, the town of his birth. He returned to the town and moved in with his parents. He was broke, homeless, and miserable. And he was still a criminal.

Lynn blamed Long for arresting him several times. On the night of July 17, 1932, both of them were in the Corner Drug Store. Lynn was drunk once again. He approached Long and said "Put 'em up, you son of a bitch. I'm going to get you sometime so it might as well be now."

With that, Long turned to see Lynn already holding a pistol on him. Long drew fast, and both men started firing. Both were struck five times. Both were moving forward as they fired.

Two bystanders were struck by Lynn's bullets. They weren't wild shots. The bullets passed through Long first. Both men survived the fight, but later died in surgery. Rody Watkins, one of the bystanders accidentally hit by the stray bullets, also died on the operating table.

And that was the end of the man who killed Marshal Tilghman and caused the Cromwell, Oklahoma, fire.

FOUR DEAD IN FIVE SECONDS

*One Dang, One Oops,
and Two Attaboys*

It was April 14, 1881. Tensions were running high in El Paso, Texas. Cattle had recently gone missing, and so did the men who went searching for those cattle. On that day, a posse of 75 armed Mexicans arrived in El Paso. They were searching for two vaqueros named Sanchez and Juarique.

Those two men had been sent to look for 30 head of stolen cattle. They hadn't been heard from in a while. The posse came to investigate.

The mayor of El Paso, Solomon Schutz, was in a quandary. He didn't want to let six dozen angry men into his city, especially since they were armed to the teeth. On the other hand, he couldn't stop them if they chose to enter. He wanted to disarm them. That was the law of the town, but he didn't have the enough men to do the job. Disarming them was impossible.

The mayor allowed them to enter. There wasn't much else he could do. He asked Gus Krempkau, a county constable, to accompany the Mexican posse.

They went directly to the Hale Ranch, owned by Johhny Hale. He was suspected of rustling cattle in the past. The Hale Ranch was 13 miles outside of the city limits of El Paso. After arriving, the posse quickly found the graves of the two missing men.

They were carried back to El Paso.

To the Americans' credit, they immediately began an inquest into the deaths. They determined that two rustlers, Pervey and Fredericks, killed them at Hale's ranch where Sanchez and Juarique had been searching for the cattle. Hale and the other rustlers feared that they would find the missing cattle and bring a search party down on the ranch.

The two rustlers had been overheard bragging about killing Sanchez and Juarique. They had been under orders to lay in wait and ambush anyone approaching the herd.

Pervey and Fredericks were formally charged with murder and arrested during the inquest. Hale and his friends were worried about what would happen next. They gathered a large crowd outside the courthouse. Among them was John Hale, suspected rustler, and his good friend and former town marshal, George Campbell.

The Americans said they were concerned that the Mexicans would become violent. The Mexicans, although armed, were very peaceful. Neither side approached the other. When the inquest was over, the Mexicans took the bodies of the two men back to Mexico for a proper funeral.

It appeared that the situation was defused. It was not.

The El Paso town marshal was Dallas Stoudenmire. He had only been on the job for three days. He wasn't from El Paso. His last job was marshal for Socorro, New Mexico. He had a reputation as a gunman. It would grow. After the inquest, he went across the street to eat dinner at the Globe Restaurant.

El Paso Marshal Dallas Stoudenmire

County Constable Gus Krempkau left his sidearms in a saloon near the courthouse. He went to retrieve his rifle and pistol. There he met the suspected rustling ringleader, John Hale and Hale's friend, retired marshal George Campbell. They began to argue.

Campbell said Krempkau was unfair with the way he translated for the Mexicans during the inquest that day. John Hale, was boisterous and drunk. He was unarmed, but suddenly he grabbed one of Campbell's guns.

"George, I've got you covered," cried Hale. Then he shot Constable Krempkau, knocking him to the ground, but not killing him. Krempkau drew his own weapon as he lay bleeding.

Marshal Stoudenmire heard the shots. He came running across the street from the restaurant, firing as he ran. Sadly, he killed an innocent bystander, a man named Ochoa.

John Hale heard the Stoudenmire shot, and he took cover behind a pillar. When he peaked out from behind it, Stoudenmire shot him between the eyes.

Campbell saw his friend Hale go down. He stepped out in the open and shouted to Stoudenmire that he did not want to fight.

The wounded Constable Krempkau, believing that it was Campbell who shot him, then fired twice at Campbell, hitting him both times.

The first bullet struck Campbell's gun. The force of the shot broke Campbell's wrist. His second shot hit him in the foot.

Stoudenmire turned from Hale and faced Campbell. Campbell with his gun hand broken scooped up his gun with his good hand. Before he could fire, Stoudenmire shot him in the stomach, and he collapsed in the street.

"You big son of a bitch. You murdered me," shouted Campbell. Stoudenmire said nothing. In a few minutes, both Campbell and Krempkau had bled to death.

All told, four men lay dead or dying after a scant five second shootout. Krempkau was killed by Hale, albeit not instantly. In less time than it takes to cross the street, Stoudenmire shot the innocent Ochoa, then Hale, and finally Campbell.

Legend says that three Texas Rangers were close by on the street but did not intervene. They later testified that they felt that Stoudenmire had everything under control.

That was the end of the famous Four Dead in Five Seconds Gunfight. It was not the end of the trouble.

A few days later, James Manning, hired Bill Johnson, a former deputy, to assassinate Marshal Stoudenmire. Johnson chose a double barreled shotgun as his weapon and hid behind a load of bricks one night.

Stoudenmire walked by. Johnson saw his chance and brought up his weapon. His mistake was being blind drunk. He stumbled, fired off both barrels, and missed. Stoudenmire emptied his pistols. In a gruesome twist of fate, he shot off Johnson's testicles, and the man bled to death in minutes.

And still, that wasn't the end. Stoudenmire continued to be challenged by Manning and his friends. On September 18, 1882, a year and a half after the famous gunfight, Stoudenmire was killed in a fight with Doc Manning and James Manning.

Marshal Stoudenmire is remembered for bringing peace to a wild town. The El Paso Police Department continues to pay tribute to him and keeps his memory alive.

NAT LOVE AND DEADWOOD DICK

Cowboy Extraordinaire

This is the story of Deadwood Dick. His real name was Nat Love. When you're talking about a rooting-tooting cowboy, you're talking about Deadwood Dick. Or Nat Love. Or both. Yeah, both.

Legend says that he was given his nickname at the 1876 Deadwood, Dakota Territory, rodeo. The nickname refers to a character that appeared in a series of penny dreadfuls or dime novels. The trouble with that "legend" is that the first story about Deadwood Dick was published on Oct 15, 1877, which is a year after the rodeo. It was published in Beadles Half-Dime Library. The author is Edward L. Wheeler.

The Deadwood Dick stories were published for the next 20 years or so. More than a few people assumed the nickname. Nat Love probably deserved it the most, even if he wasn't given the nickname a year before that moniker became associated with cowboys.

Nat was a former slave. His parents were luckier than most. His father was a foreman on a slave crew. His mother managed the kitchen. They had a slightly better life than the field hands. It was an awful life, but other slaves had it much worse.

Nat Love aka Deadwood Dick

There was a law that outlawed black literacy in the old days. Nat learned to read and write anyway. His father, Sampson, taught his three children, Sally, Jordan, and the youngest of the three, Nat.

Nat was born about 1854 in Davidson County, Tennessee, on a plantation owned by Robert Love. He was a slave until the end of the Civil War in 1865. When it ended, his family stayed in the area.

> *"The fact that I was now free gave me a newborn courage*
> *to face the world and what the future might hold for me."*
> *Nat Love aka Deadwood Dick*

His parents became sharecroppers on the Love plantation. Nat helped his parents. Sadly, his father passed away shortly afterwards. Nat stepped up. He took on a second job on another farm.

Nat had a natural affinity for horses. He rode well, and he was known for breaking horses without damaging their spirits. He didn't know it at the time, but he was setting the stage for his later exploits.

There's no doubt that Nat was a hard working son-of-a-gun. Besides working two jobs and breaking horses, he had a variety of part-time jobs to help his family. But it is always nice if luck shines upon you now and again. And shine it did on Nat.

He won a local raffle. The prize was a horse. He needed a horse, but he needed money even more. He sold the horse back to the owner for $50 and headed off to his destiny in the West. He was 16 and alone, but he had his dreams to keep him company.

He got a job when he arrived in Dodge City, Kansas. Dodge was among the most dangerous towns in the early 1870s, exactly when Nat hit town. Among the towns leading gunslingers were Wyatt Earp, Bat Masterson, and Doc Holliday.

Luckily, Nat ran into the drovers for the Duval Ranch near the Palo Duro River. They had just brought their herd to town. Nat found them while they were having breakfast. He asked the trial boss for a job. A job was offered to him, but only if he could prove himself by breaking a mean horse named Good Eye. He rode him until he gentled him. He was only 16, but his reputation was growing.

As the youngest and rawest member of the crew, Nat was given every lousy job. He learned. Before long, he was competent in all areas of cattle ranching.

Guns were necessary for a cowboy in those days. The Duval Ranch was in the middle of nowhere. The only human contact for months on end was his fellow cowboys and the occasional rustler. A cowboy has to protect the herd from danger, and that includes danger from both two- and four-legged varmints.

It was at this time that Nat became an expert marksman. It was part of his job, and he practiced until he was more than competent. Nat Love wasn't Deadwood Dick yet, but his fellow cowboys on the Duval Ranch gave him the moniker "Red River Dick."

A few years later, Nat moved on. He went to Arizona. In 1872, he took a job on the Gallinger Ranch on the Gila River. Although he had spent some time in Dodge City, Nat wrote in his autobiography that it was Arizona where he met Pat Garrett, Billy the Kid, Bat Masterson, and many other gunslingers, outlaws, and lawmen of the old West.

While working for the Gallinger Ranch, Nat was part of a cattle drive to Deadwood, Dakota Territory. Deadwood today is a city in South Dakota, and the county seat of Lawrence. It was never very large. At the time Nat visited, it probably was at its peak of about 5,000 residents.

Deadwood may have been a small town, but it boasted more than its share of gunfighters. Among them were Wyatt Earp, Calamity Jane and Wild Bill Hickok. Nat arrived in early July 1876. Just one month later, Wild Bill was shot in the back by Jack McCall. He was holding the famous "dead man's hand" of two pair, aces and eights.

Nat arrived just in time for the Fourth of July celebration. Enticed by the $200 prize money, he entered the rodeo. He won every contest and walked away with the prize for top cowboy. No one ever did that before him. No one has ever done it since.

One of his amazing feats that day was hitting 14 bull's-eyes in 14 tries at 250 yards. That would be impressive for a modern marksman. The accuracy of the average modern weapon rivals the best weapons of a century ago. But Nat did it. Fourteen bull's-eyes in a row. Wow.

Nat Love, aka Red River Dick, became an overnight sensation. The Deadwood crowd started calling him Deadwood Dick, and that became his nickname for the rest of his life.

*"By strict attention to business, born of a genuine love
of the free and wild life of the range, and absolute
fearlessness, I became known throughout the country
as a good all around cow boy and a splendid hand
in stampede." Nat Love aka Deadwood Dick*

Nat Love, also known as Red River Dick, and now Deadwood

Dick, continued his cowboy life until about 1889. Along the way, while still a cowboy, he was involved in a gunfight with Pima Indians in Arizona. He was wounded, captured, and taken to their camp. Somehow, he convinced them to spare his life. By the time he was healthy enough to leave, they respected him enough to ask him to join the tribe.

The leader of the tribe was named Yellow Dog. He wanted Nat to marry his daughter. Instead, in the dead of night, he stole a pony and escaped.

Exactly when he stopped being a cowboy is lost to history, but we know he married his wife, Alice, in 1889, and started working for the Denver and Rio Grande Railroad soon after. He took his family with them for his job, and they moved several times before settling down for good in Southern California.

His autobiography, if you can track it down, is named the Life and Adventures of Nat Love, Better Known in the Cattle Country as "Deadwood Dick, by Himself. Some say he might have added a few tall tales and stretchers, but no one really knows.

Deadwood Dick, the celebrated hero of the 1876 Deadwood Rodeo, died in Los Angeles in 1921. He was 67.

He wasn't just one of the best black cowboys of his time. He was one of the best cowboys of all time.

> *"I have seen a large part of America, and am still seeing it, but the life of a hundred years would be all too short to see our country." Nat Love aka Deadwood Dick*

ELFEGO BACA AND THE FRISCO SHOOTOUT

*Or Why a Sunken Living
Room is a Good Idea*

The story of Elfego Baca always reminds people of Judge Roy Bean, the celebrated outlaw/judge of Langtry, Texas, who called his court the "Only Law West of the Pecos."

Judge Roy wasn't a judge. Elfego Baca wasn't a lawman. That didn't stop either of them from dispensing their personal versions of Old West justice.

Elfego was born in 1865 at the close of the Civil War in Socorro, New Mexico. His family moved to Topeka, Kansas, where they lived until his mother, Juana Maria, died in 1880. At that point, his father, Francisco, took his 15-year-old son and moved back to New Mexico. This time, they settled in the small town of Belen. Francisco became a U. S. Marshal.

Four years later, Elfego somehow became a deputy sheriff in Socorro County, New Mexico. There is no record of him being appointed. Historians don't entirely agree, but most feel that

Elfego simply bought a badge and started arresting people.

"I want the outlaws to hear my steps
a block away." Elfego Baca

That part of New Mexico was sparsely populated. It was cattle country. For the most part, cowboys and others roamed free, did as they wanted, and settled their problems between themselves. That meant fights: bare knuckles brawling, knife fights, and the occasional gun battle. Elfego aimed to put a stop to such lawlessness.

One day in October 1884, Elfego arrested a drunk named Charlie McCarty. Charlie was a cowboy. He and his friends were causing minor trouble in a town called Middle San Francisco Plaza.

There were three small towns in that area of Catron County, New Mexico. All of them were called San Francisco Plaza because they were located in the San Francisco River Valley. One was called Upper San Francisco Plaza (now called Reserve, New Mexico). Another was Lower San Francisco Plaza (now Lower Frisco). The third was Middle San Francisco Plaza (now Middle Frisco).

Charlie McCarty was arrested by Elfego when he walked up wearing his badge and took his gun. That didn't sit well with Charlie's friends. They attempted to take him back by force, but Elfego wasn't having it.

Elfego Baca probably inflamed the cowboys with his heavy-handed sense of justice. When they resisted, he opened fire. There is no record of how many shots he fired or whether any of the cowboys returned fire.

What we do know is that Elfego shot one man in the knee, and another man was killed when a horse fell on him because Elfego shot it dead. The man turned out to be the foreman of John Slaughter.

John Slaughter was not a man to trifle with. He was a

lawman, cowboy and rancher. He served in the Confederate Army. He fought Indians, outlaws, rustlers. His ranch, the San Bernardino Ranch, is a National Historic Landmark in Cochise County, Arizona.

Two years after this incident and five years after the famous Gunfight at the O. K. Corral, Slaughter was elected sheriff of Cochise County. The man was hard as nails. One time, after he found he had been cheated at cards by Bryan Gallagher in San Antonio, Texas, he tracked Gallagher to New Mexico and shot him down on John Chisum's ranch.

There was no doubt that it was a wild shot that brought down the horse. The dead horse collapsed in such an odd way that the foreman standing beside the horse was somehow caught underneath the dying horse and was killed. There is no doubt about those facts. But the man killed was a friend and employee of John Slaughter. John was not happy. The situation was about to get a lot worse.

*"I never wanted to kill anybody, but if a man
had it in his mind to kill me, I made it my
business to get him first." Elfego Baca*

At this point, it becomes really important whether Elfego was appointed a lawman or whether he simply appointed himself. The local Justice of the Peace, Theodore White, declared it to be murder. He ordered the cowboy, Charlie McCarty, to be freed. He sent a messenger for local rancher Bert Hearne of the Spur Lake Ranch. When Bert arrived in town, he was made a deputy and sent to apprehend Elfego. The Frisco Shootout was about to go down.

Baca was hiding out in an adobe jacal. A jacal is a hut or building with a wooden framework covered in mud, clay, or whatever is available. In cattle country, dung is often used. This building technique is called "wattle and daub." The thickness of the walls depends on how much daub (mud) is put on the wattle (framework).

Baca's jacal was very thick. Lucky for him that it was.

Hearne came to town and ordered Elfego to surrender. He did not. Hearne repeated his order a second time and then broke down the front door. He didn't go in. He stood in front of the door and ordered him to surrender for the third time.

Elfego could be heard moving about inside, but he didn't answer. Suddenly, a volley of shots rang out. Hearne fell to the ground mortally wounded.

Elfego Baca was not safe yet. Not by a long shot. Hearne acted alone, but he was followed by a mob of cowboys. When Hearne was struck down, there were dozens of witnesses, all of them hostile to Elfego.

Witnesses later said that the cowboys numbered around 40. Elfego said it was double that amount. In any event, the cowboys wanted Elfego, and Elfego refused to surrender. No one was brave enough to approach the jacal. Hearne's body still lay where he fell.

For the next day and a half, they laid siege to the jacal. Estimates are that up to 4,000 shots were fired by the cowboys. The front door alone had more than 400 holes in it.

Elfego Baca survived without a single bullet hole. The cowboys were not so lucky. Elfego killed four of them. Eight others were injured. The gun battle ended 33 hours later when Francisquito Naranjo promised Elfego would be treated fairly.

After the Shootout, the cowboys found out why Elfego emerged without a single bullet hole. The floor to the jacal had been dug out. Upon entering the front door, visitors would have to step down to enter the main part of the jaccal. By laying low on the floor, the bullets passed harmlessly overhead.

Elfego Baca statue in Reserve, New Mexico

The Frisco Shootout happened in October of 1884. Seven months later, Elfego was officially charged with murder of John Slaughter's foreman and Deputy Bert Hearne. In August, the trial concluded. Elfego Baca was found not guilty on both counts. He was a free man.

The court found that Elfego acted within the scope of his duties as a deputy. The judge reached that decision on the basis of documents produced by Elfego's lawyer. Those papers were probably falsified. We can't know for certain, but Elfego broadly hinted at it in his autobiography.

Shortly after the Frisco Shootout, Elfego Baca became the Socorro County sheriff. Perhaps he learned his lesson from the Shootout because he did not go around indiscriminately firing his gun. Most of the men he brought to justice gave themselves up voluntarily. Many just appeared on the steps of the jail waiting for him.

What was his method to bring them in? He sent them letters stating that he was giving them time to think about it, but if they didn't surrender by a certain date, he would track them down.

"Most reports say he was the best peace officer Socorro ever had. Leon Metz, Author of The Shooters

One of his letters reads this way: "I have a warrant here for your arrest. Please come in by March 15 and give yourself up. If you don't, I'll know you intend to resist arrest, and I will feel justified in shooting you on sight when I come after you."

By 1888, four years after the Frisco Shootout, he became a U. S. Marshal. Six years after that, he passed the bar. He practiced law locally and in El Paso, Texas. He had several government jobs in Socorro County, including county clerk, mayor, school superintendent, and district attorney. He had a hand in much of the development of Socorro County, and he performed all of it very well.

> *"Leaving at once with three eyewitnesses."*
> *Elfego Baca's reply to a client's telegram asking*
> *for his help on a murder charge*

He seemed to be most interested in politics. He ran for congress in 1912 when New Mexico became a state. He lost, but he did surprisingly well with the Spanish population. This led to a relationship with New Mexico Senator Bronson Cutting. For a while, he authored a weekly column in Spanish.

For all the good that he did after the Frisco Shootout, Elfego was a troubled and unhappy man. Despite holding positions of power and authority, he kept company with the town drunks and prostitutes. He had no family life to speak of.

> *"Elfego was, and is, controversial. He drank too*
> *much; talked too much … he had a weakness*
> *for wild women." Leon Metz*

Elfego Baca, Hero (or perhaps Villain) of the Frisco Shootout, died on August 27, 1945, in Albuquerque, New Mexico. He was 80 years old and alone.

ALFERD PACKER

A Man of Exceedingly Bad Taste

Alferd (sometimes Alfred) Griner Packer was born January 21, 1842. He was one of three children. At age 20, he enlisted in the Union Army, but was released 8 months later due to epilepsy. He enlisted again. He was discharged again.

Packer wasn't a nice guy. He was known to argue, steal, and complain. The present consensus is that he was probably a pathological liar. Maybe that was why he had so many jobs: shoemaker, miner, guide, teamster, field hand, rancher. He was successful at none of them.

In 1873, he was in Utah, broke and starving. He came upon a group traveling through. Packer asked where they were going. They told him they were heading for the Colorado gold fields. Packer said he was a guide and he knew the way well.

Nope. Packer didn't know the way. At all. They followed him blindly, but quickly became uneasy with his directions and overall attitude. Packer argued with group members. Preston Nutter, one of the miners, called him a "whining fraud." He was a thoroughly disagreeable man.

Alferd Griner Packer

Packer led them generally toward Colorado, but he did not follow the best trails. Winter set upon them. Their wagons bogged down. They ran out of food. Soon they were eating horse feed and wondering if the horses themselves were next on the menu.

Luckily for them, they came upon Chief Ouray of the Utes. They were given food and shelter. The Chief advised them to stay until spring. At first, they agreed, but as they regained their strength, they wanted to move on.

The men discussed it and decided to split the party in two. Half of the party had to stay with the horses and wagons. The other half, 10 men plus Packer, decided to push on. The idea was to travel to the Los Pinos Indian Agency and then to their destination, Breckenridge, Colorado. The Utes tried to discourage them, but they were determined to leave.

Chief Ouray advised the group to follow the Gunnison River. Packer said he knew a quicker way through the mountains. Half of the group, 5 men, followed Chief Ouray's advice and followed the river. The remaining 5 men decided to let Packer guide them through the mountains. They had food for two weeks, but they were not outfitted for mountain travel. They left on February 9.

On April 16, 1874, Packer stumbled into the Los Pinos Indian Agency near Saguache, Colorado. He was alone. They fed him. He told his story. He said he went snow blind and the party abandoned him with one rifle and almost no food.

*Memorial to the Victims of Alferd
Packer in Lake City, Colorado*

The men at the Indian Agency later said that Packer didn't look malnourished at all. In fact, he looked a bit chubby. That seemed a bit suspicious, but there wasn't a hint as to what actually happened.

Packer hung around Saguache, Colorado, where he began drinking and spending money. He told his story many times, and he kept changing it. No one believed him.

Around this time, several of the members of his original group walked into Packer's favorite bar, the Dolan's Saloon. These members had wintered with Chief Ouray. They had plenty of questions for him.

Why did he look so well fed? Why would the miners abandon him if he was the only one who knew the way? Why would they give Packer one of their only rifles? Why did Packer have one of the miner's knives? And most damning of all, where did the previously broke Packer get all the money he was spending at the saloon and in stores?

The men were irate. Many called for Packer to be lynched right then and there. Cooler heads insisted that he be turned over to authorities. An officer from the Indian Agency arrived during their quarrel and insisted that Packer return with him to the agency.

When they arrived, Packer was questioned. He denied everything until two Ute hunters arrived with strips of human flesh that they had found near the agency. Packer confessed. Sort of.

Packer said the other men killed the first miner, Israel Swan, but he reluctantly joined them in butchering and eating the man. He said that they shared the man's money and belongings. Then they killed another, and another, and another. Each time, they would divide up the money and possessions among a smaller and smaller group.

Finally it was just Packer and a man named Shannon Bell. Packer said he was forced to kill Bell in self-defense. He butchered the body, ate what he could, and packed up the rest for the journey.

That was Packer's first version of the events. He had several.

The bodies were found that summer by an illustrator for Harper's Weekly magazine. They were just two miles from Lake City, Colorado. All of them had been killed about the same time. The bodies were in various stages of butchering. Packer's story didn't match what they found.

Packer was jailed. He escaped. He was jailed again. He changed his story again. The new version had Shannon Bell killing the other men at one time, and Packer killing Bell again in self-defense.

Packer was tried, convicted, and sentenced to hang. There was a technical point that caused that conviction to be overturned. He was tried a second time. He was convicted of five counts of manslaughter and sentenced to 40 years. He served 18 years and was pardoned. He lived a quiet and unremarkable life for his remaining years.

In 1968, in a stroke of unbelievably bad taste, the University of Colorado at Boulder renamed their cafeteria, the Alferd G. Packer Memorial Grill. Their motto is "Have a friend for lunch."

Yuck.

THE DONNER PARTY

When All the Choices Were Horrible

The one big distinction between Alferd Packer and the Donner Party is that the Donner Party was truly starving. No one doubts that. It's hard to justify eating human flesh for any reason. If there is a reason, though, the Donner Party had it. They encountered extraordinary bad luck, along with a bad choice of routes and insufficient training and supplies.

The pioneers in the Donner Party were mostly families that were traveling together by chance. Before they came to the mountains, they splintered off from other wagon trains. Some of them were fairly well off. Others were barely scraping by. None were prepared for what lay ahead.

In early 1846, a large train, estimated at 500 wagons, left Independence, Missouri. Among them were 32 members of the Donner and Reed families, along with their employees and nine wagons. Soon after, they left this train and joined up with a smaller one of 50 wagons led by William Russell. Other families also joined this wagon train.

James and Margret Reed

The beginning and middle of the long trip was relatively easy and uneventful. The hard part was the last 100 miles. It was entirely in the Sierra Nevada mountains. Being close to the Pacific coast, this range is known for heavy snowfalls. The trick to crossing it was to leave after the spring thaw and before the first snows of the fall. Start out too early, and the wagons would be stuck in mud. Start too late, and there would be the danger of heavy snow.

A man named Lansford Hastings claimed to have a better and safer route through the mountains. It was called the Hastings Cutoff. To promote his guide services, he sent riders east to meet the approaching pioneers. The Donners and their wagon train met one of these riders. They were instructed to meet Hastings at Fort Bridger, Wyoming, if they wanted his guidance.

Most of the wagon train opted to stay on the main trail. A smaller group, including the Donners, headed to Fort Bridger. Jim Bridger, the famous scout and frontiersman, ran a small supply depot there. What he did to the Donners borders on the criminal.

A man named Edwin Bryant and a small group scouted ahead of the wagon train. They reached Fort Bridger a week before the Donners and continued on to the Hastings Cutoff. They found it to be rough going, even at the start. Bryant sent word back by letter warning the Donners to return to the main route. The Hastings Cutoff passed through the Wasatch Range, went across the Great Salt Lake Desert, skirted the Ruby Mountains, and then rejoined the California Trail.

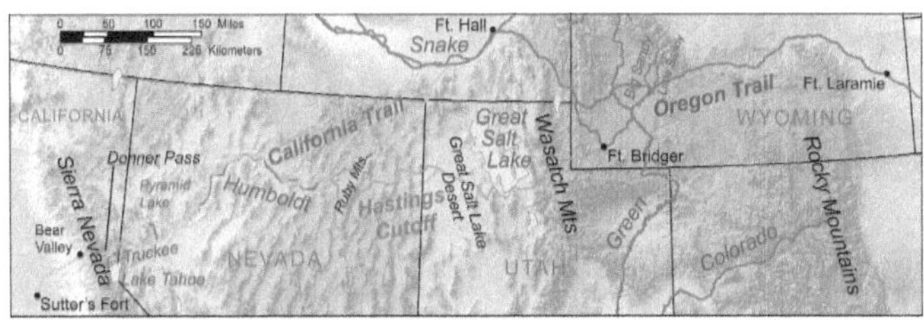

*Map of the Donner Party route, including
the Hastings Cutoff*

Bridger hid the letter from them. Instead he advised them that the new route was easy to cross by wagon with plentiful water and no hostile Indians. To be fair, he did advise them of a 40 mile stretch of desert salt flats that they would have to cross. Even that was a lie. It was a painful 80 miles that took 6 days. At the end of those 6 days, they had lost oxen, cows, mules and wagons. Some collapsed from the heat and lack of water. Some went crazy with thirst and bolted off into the desert.

The Hastings Cutoff was supposed to save them 350 miles of travel. Instead it cost them a precious month of time, some of their wagons and a good part of their stock.

*"The most direct route, for the California emigrants,
would be to leave the Oregon route, about two hundred
miles east from Fort Hall; thence bearing West
Southwest, to the Salt Lake; and thence continuing
down to the bay of St. Francisco, by the route just
described." Description from the Hastings Handbook*

The wagon train was already weary from the trip, and they had not yet reached the Sierra Nevadas. They were getting frustrated. They argued with each other. Their animals were weak from the desert. The grass was thinning with the approaching winter. To lighten the burden on the animals, the pioneers walked as much as possible.

One poor soul, 70-year-old John Snyder Hardkoop, was traveling alone. When he was told to walk, he tried for three days. Then he sat down and watched them travel out of sight. No one stopped. No one helped him. They said they were exhausted and they could not help.

The final stretch of the desert found them besieged by Indians. They stole their horses and cattle, including oxen. Several more wagons had to be abandoned. Those without wagons could only carry so much food, and they soon ran out. They were all in bad shape, and no one would help the weak for fear of dying themselves.

Great Salt Lake Desert

Once they crossed the final section of desert, they were at the Truckee River. Two men, Charles Stanton and William McCutchen had gone ahead to Sutter's Fort, California, hoping to get aid from John Sutter of the famous Sutter's Mill gold strike. They reached him exhausted and emaciated.

Stanton came back with mules and supplies, although not nearly enough. By this time it was mid-October. Snow had already fallen, but they expected the pass to still be open for travel. It was not.

They tried several times to make it over the pass. They found snow drifts up to ten feet high, and they couldn't find the trail. Each time they were forced to return to a lower elevation, but they were still high in the mountains.

They were determined to move forward. By the time they

realized they couldn't cross the pass, the path behind them was also snowed over. They were stuck there for the winter. It was miserable.

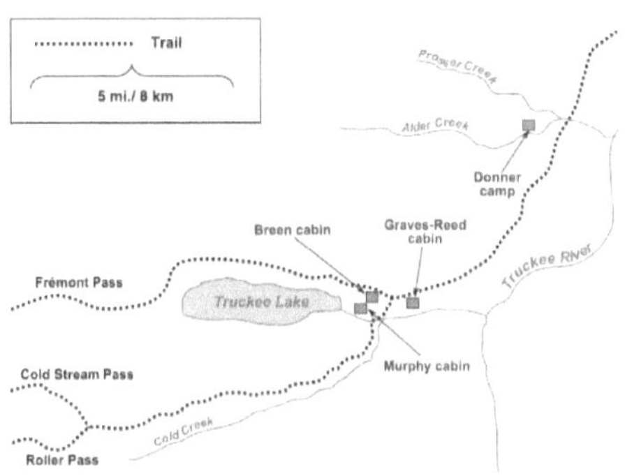

*Location of the main shelters at Truckee
Lake and Alder Creek*

They built crude cabins without doors or windows. Canvas or ox hides covered the openings and roofs. Later, when they were emaciated and near death, they would eat the hides, along with any leather including shoes, vests, coats, etc.

Seventeen of them decided to walk over the pass. They became lost. They didn't know the way over the pass or back to camp. They starved. This is when they first considered cannibalism. Some said one of the group should make the sacrifice voluntarily. Others suggested a lottery.

In the end, they simply waited until someone died. Three were dead before they found the courage to begin eating the corpses. On January 12, they stumbled into a Miwok camp. The Miwoks fed them and took one to a farm. A rescue party was sent for the others. Seventeen had started the trip over the pass. Ten died.

It took them a little more than a month, but finally, word had reached California that the Donner Party was stranded in the mountains.

Throughout the journey, the Donner Party encountered bad

luck at every turn. Now with the authorities in California aware of the trapped pioneers, the rescued men expected an expedition would be mounted to save the rest of the group. That did not happen. The Mexican-American War was raging on. The military had its hands full.

A private rescue party started out on February 4. Two weeks later, they made it to the crude cabins used by the pitiful wagon train. Thirteen were dead. Several were exhibiting psychological problems. Many were injured, dying, or too weak to travel.

The rescue party brought food and supplies. They chose 23 of the strongest and began the trip out of the mountains. Thirty-three were left behind. The strong were not very strong. Several died on the trip. At one point, they went several days without food. Rescuers reported the survivors began eating any leather they could find.

Eventually, they made it out of the mountains. One man, William Hook, was so crazed with hunger that he gorged himself on foodstuffs and promptly died. On the final part of the trip to Sutter's Fort, they passed the second rescue mission.

"I really thought I had stepped over into paradise." 12-year-old Virginia Reed upon reaching Sutter's Fort.

The second rescue expedition found that cannibalism was still ongoing. Some were ashamed and threw away evidence as soon as they saw the rescuers. Others did not attempt to hide it. As an example, when they found Elizabeth Donner, wife of Jacob, she refused to eat the only meat available, but she fed it to her children. It was her husband, Jacob. The rescuers found that three other corpses had been eaten as well.

I wish I could cry but I cannot. If I could forget
the tragedy, perhaps I would know how
to cry again." Mary Graves

A third rescue party arrived on March 14. One of the rescuers, William Eddy, found that his son had been eaten by one of the survivors, Lewis Keseberg. He vowed to kill him if he saw him in California. The rescuers left with four children. Keseberg remained there in the mountains.

The next few attempts were aborted due to weather. The next one to reach the Donner Party thought they would not find anyone alive. George Donner passed away just a few days before they arrived.

Keseberg was found alive and with a pot full of human flesh. He had George Donner's pistols, jewelry and money. The rescuers threatened to hang him, but he was brought back to Sutter's Fort. He was the last person rescued.

"I have not wrote to you half the trouble we have had but I have wrote enough to let you know that you don't know what trouble is. But thank God we have all got through and the only family that did not eat human flesh. We have left everything but I don't care for that. We have got through with our lives but Don't let this letter dishearten anybody. Never take no cutoffs and hurry along as fast as you can." Virginia Reed, survivor

Keseberg later sued several members of the final rescue party for implying that he had killed Tamsen Donner, wife of George Donner, shortly before being found by the third rescue party. The court awarded him a mere $1, but he was ordered to pay court costs.

*Trees cut by the Donner Party. Height of the stumps gives
an idea of the depth of the snow. Photo taken in 1866.*

Eighty-seven people started the trip. Forty-eight survived.
There was, initially, a great deal of sympathy for the Donner
Party. The details were well known. As time passed, only the
cannibalism was remembered.

It is clear from their stories and recovered evidence that the
pioneers desperately tried to avoid cannibalism. They ate their
animals, including pets. They boiled and ate shoes, jackets,
hides. They boiled bones until the bones became so brittle that
they broke. Then they crushed the bones and ate them as a
mush.

Only some of the survivors ate human flesh. Many of the
survivors did not. Would more have survived if they resorted to
cannibalism? If some survived without cannibalism, did any of
them need to do so?

Estimates of the cannibalism range up to twenty-one bodies
being at least partially eaten. No one can know for sure. There is
the oral evidence given by the survivors and the eyewitness accounts by rescue crews.

Here is a very hard question: If you were in the same situation, would you choose to starve to death or eat human flesh?

Here is a harder question: If your children were starving,

would you feed them human flesh?

Those are horrible horrible situations. The survivors spent their lives haunted by what they had done.

THE PONY EXPRESS

Connecting the East and the West

The Pony Express is firmly embedded in the history of the American West. Even today, the image of a lone rider galloping across the desert chased by marauding Indians immediately conjures up stories of the Pony Express.

TV shows and movies about the Pony Express always, always, always have at least one scene of Express riders running for their lives, usually across the desert. It makes for exciting viewing for the Saturday matinee crowd, but it's not as typical as one may think.

In truth, there was trouble with the Paiutes for a short period of time. The underlying cause is unclear. Blame is given to both sides, and it did result in a minor delay of the mail. So there is a kernel of truth to the "Pony Express rider galloping for his life" movie scenes. There just isn't very much more than a kernel of truth. And a small kernel at that.

For the most part, the Pony Express riders were extremely hard working men who rode an almost absurd number of miles each day. It wasn't pleasant. In fact, after just a few trips, it became dull, boring, and exhausting. The one saving grace was that it paid very well.

Pony Express Poster with mailing rates and schedule

The short life of the Pony Express began on April 3, 1860. It remained in operation for a mere 18 months. The telegraph replaced it when it came into operation in October 1861. Until that happened, the Pony Express was a vital link with the far West. Pioneers were flooding in. Towns were established. States were created. Gold was found in California. The West was exploding in population, industry, and money. There was a great need for faster communication.

Three men conceived the Pony Express in the 1850s. They were William Russell, William Waddell, and Alexander Majors. All of them were partners in short- and long-haul freighting. Part of their business was supplying the U. S. Army out West. One partner, Russell, came up with the idea for quick mail delivery. They wanted the same kind of contracts for mail delivery that they had for freight. That didn't happen, but they went ahead with their plans.

Postmark of the Pony Express

In the East, telegraphs were common in the cities. The Pony Express could not compete with the telegraph. The Pony Express extended only as far East as St. Joseph, Missouri. At that point, mail was traditionally carried by stagecoach to the Western states.

The Pony Express had two distinct advantages over the stagecoach. A single rider was much faster than a stage coach with passengers and freight. A rider on horse could use shortcuts that would be impassable for a stagecoach.

It took them a short two months to put together the initial route. They used way stations, farms, abandoned buildings. If they couldn't find a suitable building, they built one. By February 1861, they had a complete system, including riders and horses.

I, ... , do hereby swear, before the Great and Living
God, that during my engagement, and while I am an
employee of Russell, Majors, and Waddell, I will, under
no circumstances, use profane language, that I will drink
no intoxicating liquors, that I will not quarrel or fight
with any other employee of the firm, and that in every
respect I will conduct myself honestly, be faithful to my
duties, and so direct all my acts as to win the confidence
of my employers, so help me God. Pony Express Oath

The riders had to swear to be respectable and faithful in their duties. They promised not to swear, drink, or fight while employed by the Pony Express. They had to sign the official oath. They were also given a Bible. It was small and lightweight. It gave them something to read when they were resting in an out-of-the-way station far from civilization.

There were strict requirements for the riders. They had to weigh 125 pounds or less. Less was better. The rider's only job was to stay on the back of the horse. The lighter the man, the lighter the burden on the horse.

The total weight that was allowed on each horse was 165 pounds. That included everything including the saddle and the mail. The mail wasn't strapped down. They used something very similar to ordinary saddlebags, except there were two pouches on each side, one in front of the leg and one behind the leg. Each of those pouches were very small. These saddlebags would fit perfectly over top of the saddle. It would be held in place by the weight of the rider. They were called mochilas, which is Spanish for "pouch."

Stations with corrals, horses, food, and beds were established at varying distances. In rough or mountainous country, they were closer together. In flatland, deserts, or on good roads, they were farther apart.

The St. Joseph, Missouri, Pony Express Stables

Riders almost exclusively rode one leg in one direction each day. In a pinch, a rider may be given an immediate trip back or told to continue on to the next station. That was an immense hardship and could require a rider to stay in saddle for close to a full day.

The name "pony" is a hard rascal to nail down. It can mean a particular type of horse or a horse of a specific size. Not all of the horses used by the Pony Express were truly ponies by anybody's definition, but all of them were small, compact, and able to run at top speed for long periods of time.

Horses that were faster did not have the endurance. Those with better endurance were slower. Ponies, or horses with similar characteristics, were the best choice. Just like the riders, they were pushed to their limits, but they performed admirably.

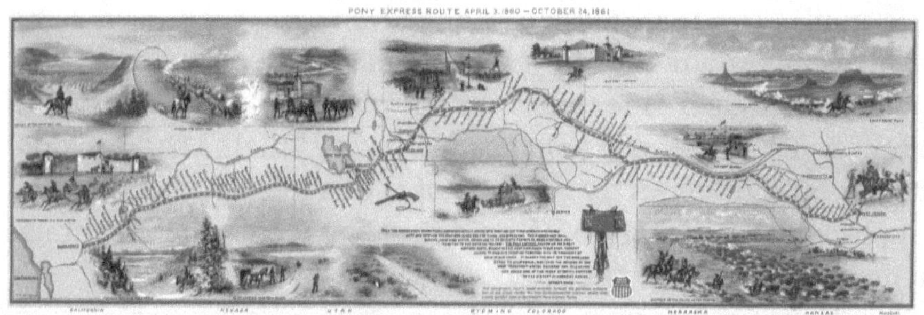

Pony Express route 1860

The full route from St. Joseph, Missouri, to Sacramento, California, was 1,900 miles. Mail was guaranteed to be delivered in ten days or less. The trail loosely followed established wagon trails. They used the Oregon and California trails. Part of the trip went through Fort Bridger and the Hastings Cutoff, both of which were famous for their role in the Donner Party incident. They went through established towns like Carson City, Nevada, and Salt Lake City, Utah. They took whatever route was the quickest.

As much as possible, the routes would go through or near cities and towns along the way. Riders went through Fort Kearny, Nebraska, Gothenburg, Nebraska, Chimney Rock, Colorado, and many other small towns.

*Billy Richardson, Johnny Fry, Charles Cliff
and Gus Cliff -- Four of the best riders*

In general, a day's ride would be 75 to 100 miles. Stations were set up along the route. At each station, horses were exchanged for fresh ones. Riders were expected to stop only to long enough to slap their mail pouch on the fresh horse. No resting, eating, or outhouse usage. Gallop in; gallop out. Keep eating up the miles.

The stations at the end of their daily routes had food, beds, and perhaps a bit of medicine. One can only assume that saddle sores were a big problem. Riders were exhausted at first, but they rapidly became used to the regimen.

On April 3, 1860, two riders departed with the mail. One left from Sacramento, California. The other left from St. Joseph, Missouri. True to their promises, the Pony Express delivered both pouches of mail within their ten-day guarantee. The Pony Express was barely in business, and it was already a rousing success.

No one knows for sure who the first rider was. There are two candidates: Billy Richardson and Johnny Fry. Both of those riders were in St. Joseph. Because of the time difference, the westbound mail started out before the eastbound mail in Sacramento.

Postmark from the first westbound trip

The Pony Express earned an extraordinary reputation for delivering their mail on time. However, almost from the start, they encountered a serious problem. Just one month after mail delivery started, there was a series of relatively minor incidents called the Paiute War. The Paiutes had endured a hard winter. Some say they were planning war for quite some time. Others say there were no such plans.

In any event, a party of Indians burned a Pony Express station on the Carson River in Nevada. One explanation for the attack was simply that the Paiutes wanted to go to war. Another explanation is that the Paiutes had heard about two Paiute women being kept against their will at the station. They went to investigate and a fight broke out. No one really knows the reasoning behind the attack.

The Paiutes killed the five men at the station. It was only the beginning. Over the next month or so, the Paiutes raided isolated farms and ranches. The Pony Express stations were favorite targets. Each one had a stable of fine horses and very little defense against attack. In total, 16 men were killed, and whopping 150 horses were taken.

This violence caused the one and only delay of the mail. Luckily, it was a brief war, and soon the Pony Express was back in full operation. From that point, there was no further trouble as far as the Pony Express was concerned. Many historians note that attacks on private individuals or isolated businesses were relatively rare. The great majority of conflict was between the Army and the Native Americans.

The cost to send a letter was exorbitant, but it was the only way to get a letter across the country so quickly. Initially, the price was set at $5 per half ounce. As time went by, the price dropped. At the end, it was only $1 per half ounce, but that was still very expensive. The telegraph cut down the need for the Pony Express and eventually replaced it as the best and most efficient way to communicate coast to coast.

William Russell, the partner who initially conceived the idea of the Pony Express came up with an exceptional way to advertise it. Russell hired extra riders and extra horses which he strung out along the route to Sacramento. The telegraph lines had reached as far west as Fort Kearny, Nebraska. That became the starting point for his publicity stunt.

When he received word of the 1860 presidential election, he dispatched the news by Pony Express. The news of Lincoln's election reached California a mere seven days after it happened. That was unheard of at the time.

Pony Express riders Billy Richardson,
Johnny Fry, Charlels Cliff, Gus Cliff

It was a huge feather in the cap of the Pony Express. They deserved the fame and goodwill that they earned with their superior mail service. Trouble was on the way though. In less than a year, the telegraph would spell the end of the Pony Express.

A very young William Cody was their most famous rider, but he earned most of his fame later as a scout and frontiersman. He had not yet earned the nickname of Buffalo Bill. That would come later during the Civil War. He joined the Pony Express as just another scrawny 15-year-old kid who said he could ride. They put him to work constructing stations at first.

William "Buffalo Bill" Cody

Soon, they gave him his first route. It was a relatively easy 45-mile run. After proving himself capable, he was given a very hard route in Wyoming. He once made a round trip ride of 322 miles without stopping. It took 21 hours and required almost two dozen horses.

Wild Bill is known today as the most famous Pony Express

rider, but he wasn't back then. That honor went to Robert Haslam aka Pony Bob.

Pony Bob was one of the riders during the publicity stunt carrying news of Lincoln's victory to the West Coast. He rode his route to Buckland's Station. When he got there, he found that the next rider refused to ride due to the threat of Indian trouble. Pony Bob took the mail and headed off. He completed that leg of the trip for a total of 190 miles for the day.

After a night's rest, he took the eastbound mail back the way he came. At the first rest station, he found that the station master was dead and Indians had run off with the horses. He kept going and made it back to where he started. The total mileage for that trip was an astounding 380 miles.

Pony Express statue in St. Joseph, Missouri

One of the almost unknown riders was young Billy Tate. While on his route, fourteen-year-old Billy was chased by Paiutes. He hid in some rocks and engaged in a shootout. He killed seven before they got to him. Billy wasn't scalped. That was seen as a sign of respect from the Paiutes.

Another misconception about the Pony Express is that they rode their horses flat out at full gallop. The horses wouldn't have been able to keep up that pace. The riders varied the speed, but kept it at a fast trot or above unless the horse was injured. Yes, sometimes, they were at a full gallop. But no, they couldn't push their horses that hard all the time.

For all of its successes and accolades, the Pony Express was a dismal failure financially. It lost more than twice as much money as it made. Nonetheless, it is one of the most storied chapters in American history.

1874 LOCUST PLAGUE AND THE ROCKY MOUNTAIN LOCUST

Locusts, grasshoppers, or just plain hoppers plagued America for decades before we learned how to mitigate the horrific damage they caused. We can lessen the harm, but so far, we haven't been able to eliminate it. In 2019, Nevada suffered a devastating invasion of locusts. Las Vegas received the worst of it. Throughout all the years and all the locust plagues, one particular time has always stood out as the absolute worst. That time was a short week and a half in 1874.

The Rocky Mountain locust is now extinct, but they were once the scourge of the Old West. One swarm in 1875 was estimated to cover an area larger than California with an amazing 12.5 trillion insects. That swarm was named Albert's Swarm after Albert Child, a physician, who calculated the size of the swarm by its speed and the time it took to pass his location.

Less than thirty years later, they were gone.

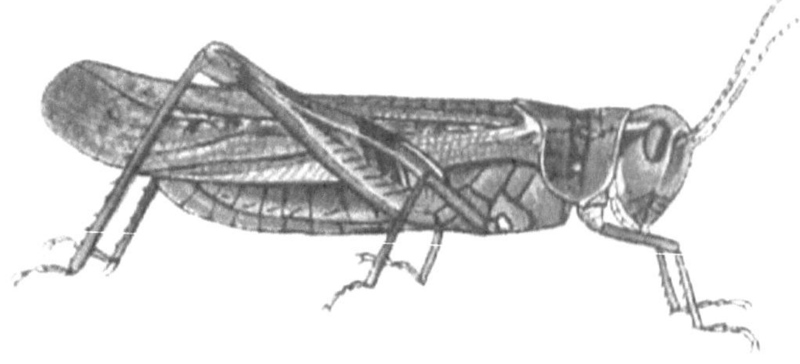

Rocky Mountain locust, Melanoplus Spretus

Another locust, the High Plains locust, became a similar crop pest in the 1930s. It is not extinct, but its numbers have been greatly reduced.

Locusts are basically grasshoppers that migrate. That's pretty much the definition. If they remained in one area, they wouldn't be nearly as devastating.

Initially, in the 1700s, the locusts caused crop damage in the New England states with several outbreaks reported. As America expanded, so did the farmland. Plagues doubled and tripled in occurrences and in their size. Between 1856 and 1874, some areas, such as Kansas and Nebraska, suffered infestations every year.

(It was) like a great white cloud, like a snowstorm,
blocking out the sun like vapor. Unidentified Farmer

The eleven days of July 20 to July 30, 1874, are known as the worst days of the invasion. The locusts ate everything, not just crops and grass. Leather, wood, canvas, paper, clothing were eaten by the swarming hoppers. There were reports of people caught outside who found their clothing in shreds.

Farmers tried various methods to save their crops. None were ultimately successful. Setting fires was probably the most effective, but only minimally and at great cost.

Funny contraptions were invented to knock down, squash, poison, vacuum or somehow kill locusts. They didn't work. The farmers made valiant efforts, but ultimately to no avail. You had to admire their ingenuity. They tried.

Merriam Webster still lists the word "hopperdozer." Its definition is: a device for catching and destroying insects (as grasshoppers) that is drawn on runners across a field and has a shield against which insects jump and fall into a pan containing kerosene or oil.

In general, it was thought that outbreaks lasted two years. The locusts would descend from the mountains and wreak havoc on the plains. They could survive and reproduce away from the mountains, but the hatchlings suffered a high mortality rate. The eggs and hatchlings weren't suited to the plains, and they did not adapt.

The perfect habitat was the dry, high altitude regions of the eastern slope of the Rockies. Any lower than 2,000 feet was too moist for them to reproduce in any numbers.

Rocky Mountain locusts sharing a meal in 1870

The 1874 plague was the largest and most devastating. The Great Plains lost virtually all crops. People were starving. That may be why Charles Riley came up with a recipe. Simply pan fry the rascals and salt and pepper to taste. Mr. Riley was an entomologist. He probably found the recipe more palatable than most people.

In the late 1870s, state governments passed laws or started programs to control the locusts. Nebraska passed an 1877 law that said each man had to work two days to kill locusts or face a fine. Missouri paid bounties for bushels of locusts.

When the plague was over, the Great Plains quickly recovered. New crops were introduced, such as winter wheat which is harvested before locusts can swarm. Some other agricultural practices were changed to limit the damage from future swarms.

And then they were gone. Why it happened is a mystery. They devastated American crops in the early 1870s, particularly 1874, but the last reported sighting of a Rocky Mountain locust was in 1902.

Like horror movie villains, some predict the Rocky Mountain locust will reappear in the future when the conditions are right. Some say that all it will take is a slight change in the environment to bring them back.

Keep your fingers crossed.

JOAQUIN MURRIETA, THE ROBIN HOOD OF THE WEST

Joaquin Murrieta Carrillo is a man of mystery. We know that he became a California outlaw during the Gold Rush. We don't know why. There is much speculation, but it is purely speculation. We know that he was a vaquero (cowboy) and a gold miner in Mexico. When he came to California, he picked up gold mining again.

*Joaquin, the Mountain Robber, circa
1848, by an unknown artist*

Whatever happened after that turned him into one of the most wanted men in California.

Joaquin Murrieta Carillo was born in Sonora, Mexico, about 1829. He grew up there. By 1849, he was married to Rosa Feliz. His stepbrother, Joaquin Carrillo, was in California. The Gold Rush had just started. Murrieta and his extended family were invited to move to California. A dozen or more accompanied Murrieta.

The most popular story of how he became a bandit says that he and his stepbrother were accused of stealing a mule. He was whipped. His stepbrother was hanged. His wife was raped and killed. Murrieta swore revenge and spent the next several years tracking down his enemies.

Some of that is possibly true. It is also possible that he simply turned to crime for the money. In any event, he hadn't been in California long before he and his relatives formed the Five Joaquins Gang.

Legend says that the gang was created to track down those who had killed his stepbrother and raped his wife. As with all the other speculation about Murrieta, while that is possible, there is no solid proof. What we know for sure is that the Five Joaquins Gang rapidly got involved in illegal horse trading and widespread murder. As many as forty-one miners were killed. Most of them were Chinese.

In May 1853, California created and hired 20 California State Rangers for the express purpose of tracking down the Five Joaquins. The Rangers were seasoned veterans of the Mexican-American War. They were led by Harry Love, former Texas Ranger. They were promised $1,000 by the governor if they captured the gang.

Two months later, the Rangers engaged a band of Mexicans in a shootout. Three were killed. One was said to be Murrieta. Another was Three-Fingered Jack. Two other men were captured. Not much is known about Jack, except for what happened after he was killed.

To collect the reward, the Rangers had to have proof. A photographer wasn't available. Carrying the bodies to Sacramento wasn't practical in the July heat. The Rangers decided to cut off Murrieta's head and Three-Fingered Jack's hand. They placed the body parts in alcohol and brought them to the authorities to collect their reward.

After collecting the reward, the Rangers put them on tour throughout California. For $1, spectators could view the head and hand.

Just one month after Murrieta was killed, the first of many myths came to light. There was a claim that the Rangers killed innocent victims and passed them off as the Five Joaquins Gang. Another claim was that the people who identified Murrieta's head were paid off. Seventeen people signed affidavits identifying his head. One was a Catholic priest.

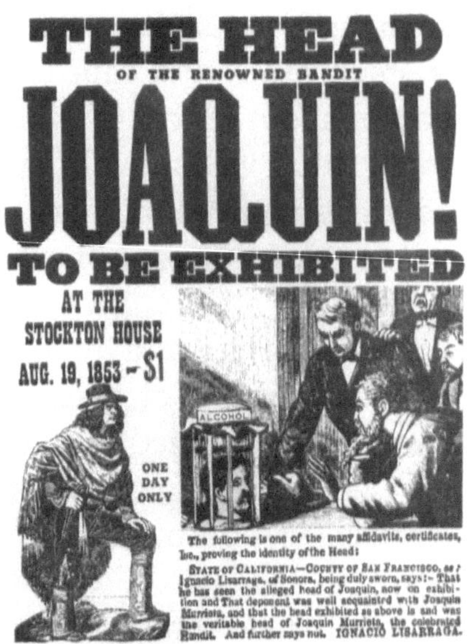

*1853 poster advertising the exhibition
of the head of Joaquin Murrieta*

A second claim was that Murrieta's head was never displayed in the mining camps where he was known. This was proven to be untrue, but it added to the confusion between fact and fiction.

Many years later, in 1870, Murrieta's sister was heard to say the head was not her brother's. Other reports had Murrieta spotted as an old man. None were ever confirmed.

Most likely, the Rangers actually killed Murrieta as they claimed. He was never seen again, except for a few unsubstantiated sightings. But can we say for certain? No. Maybe he decided to quit his banditry and moved to another state to live quietly.

As with many of the mysteries of the Old West, we will never know the truth, but that is okay. The myths and legends are always entertaining.

THE US CAMEL CORPS AND THE LEGEND OF RED GHOST

One Lump or Two?

The US Army began investigating the use of camels as far back as the 1830s. They wanted to use them out West. They conducted studies. The recommendations were always the same. Camels would be perfect as pack animals in the hot, arid environment of the American Southwest.

Despite the recommendations, the Army continually turned down the idea until Jefferson Davis became Secretary of War. He had always liked the project. As soon as he was put in office in 1853, he advocated the use of camels. Congress was a little slow, but in 1855, they finally appropriated $30,000 for the creation of the US Camel Corps.

Major Henry C. Wayne was given the job of purchasing the camels. Major Wayne had done a study in 1848 about using camels. He knew what was required, and he was a very hands-on man. He sailed to Egypt, Turkey, Greece and a few more countries and personally bought camels, saddles, and equipment. He even hired five camel drivers. Then he sailed for Texas. On this trip, he brought 34 camels.

Camel at Drum Barracks, San Pedro, California

On May 14, 1856, they reached Indianola, Texas. Major Wayne took the camels to Camp Verde, Texas. He sent his second in command, Lieutenant David Porter, back to sea to acquire more camels. Porter came back the next year with 41 more.

One of the first missions of the Camel Corps was a long trip in 1857 from Camp Verde to Fort Defiance. Along the way, they would travel through San Antonio, Fort Davis, El Paso, and Albuquerque.

The leader of the expedition was Lieutenant Edward Beale. Beale loaded each camel with 600 pounds of gear and supplies. He reportedly wrote that he would rather have one camel than four mules.

Based on the success of this mission, Congress was asked to purchase 1,000 camels. They turned it down. Politicians can be stubborn.

Two years later, in 1859, the Army sent 24 camels and 24 mules on a mission to reconnaissance the Pecos River/Rio Grande area. On June 15, they set out on a long slow trip through the desert. The first leg was about 85 miles. The camels were given no water until they finished. The second part was over

110 miles. At the end of the trip, the mules were worn out, but the camels were healthy.

Each time that the Army tested the camels, they found that the camels were better than mules, horses, or oxen in the desert and arid regions. The evidence was mounting. Congress was expected to reconsider their decision about expanding the Camel Corps

Well, that was what everybody expected, but then the Civil War came around. The Southwest was largely forgotten as the North and South battled it out mainly in the eastern half of America.

In the middle of the Civil War, the Army decided to abandon the project. Part of the reason may have been resentment against Jefferson Davis and Robert E. Lee. Before the Civil War, both had voiced strong support for the Camel Corps.

Probably the biggest reason was that Americans just weren't familiar with camels. Anyone who worked with camels was enthusiastic in their support, but those less familiar with them were decidedly against camels.

One good example of the prejudice against camels was an attempt to use them to deliver mail between two Army posts. One post was Fort Mohave (originally Camp Colorado) in the New Mexico Territory. The other was Camp Drum (Drum Barracks) built during the Civil War to protect Los Angeles. The camels performed very well, but both commanders complained to their superiors. They got their wish. The camels were removed.

Camels did have their downside. They didn't get along very well with horses and mules. The soldiers that worked with them said that they stank to high heaven. Many of the newer, inexperienced drivers complained about the difficulty of controlling the camels.

Eventually the US Army said enough is enough. They sold off the camels in their possession in 1864. Early in the war, February 28, 1861, Camp Verde and its camels were captured by the Confederacy. After the camp was recaptured in 1865, there were 100 or more camels in the camp or the surrounding countryside.

The Army was able to sell off the camels. The largest group went to Bethel Coopwood, a Texas lawyer and judge. He bought 66 of the beasts in hopes of turning a profit reselling them.

The camels ended up in some unlikely places. Some were sold to circuses. Others were used for their novelty at fairs and rodeos. Camel races and camel rides became a familiar sight. And some of them actually were put to work by miners and tradesmen.

And that was that. The Camel Corps was no more. It lasted a scant 10 years, 1856-1866. After it was officially disbanded and the stock was sold off, a few wild camels were seen in the area. The last one was in 1875. There were reports of other sightings. Most of those sightings were due to the camels being abandoned by their owners. They simply are not easy to handle. In 1885, when General Douglas MacArthur was five years old, he saw one at Fort Seldon, New Mexico. Reported sightings continued for decades. The last one in captivity was Topsy. She died in a Los Angeles zoo in 1934. The last one in the wild may have lived into the 1940s

Wait, the story isn't done yet.

The US Army wasn't alone in using camels. The Confederates used them too. The most famous one was Old Douglas of Company A of the 43rd Mississippi Infantry. Jefferson Davis continued to promote camels after he became the President of the Confederacy, and Old Douglas was one of the first they acquired.

After the war, Old Douglas ended up on Jefferson Davis' farm where he spent his remaining years.

Wait, wait, wait. We're still not done.

All of this camel business spawned the Legend of the Red Ghost. There were various accounts. Some said it was a ferocious beast with a silent, armed rider. A story in the Smithsonian reported a legend of a ghost that killed a bear and that could disappear into thin air.

The Red Ghost was finally caught and killed. He was snacking in a rancher's vegetable patch. It was a camel with reddish hair.

And now we're done.

COLTER'S RUN

With a Little Help from the Beavers

John Colter is generally known as the first of the mountain men. He was a member of the Lewis and Clark Expedition, partly because of his hunting skills and partly as a scout. He was also admired for his ability to negotiate with Native Americans using only hand gestures. He was praised by President Thomas Jefferson for his work on the expedition.

Colter was the first European to see the area that we now know as the Yellowstone and Grand Teton Nation Parks. When he returned to civilization, no one believed his reports of geysers, superheated pools of water and mud pots (similar to a superheated spring or pool, but mostly boiling mud).

He was born to explore. In late 1807, he ventured into the wilds with his rifle and a fairly heavy backpack (perhaps up to 40 pounds). He intended to establish a relationship with the Crow Nation for future trading. He spent that winter hiking through the West in deep snow and freezing temperatures. The stories he told about his trip earned him ridicule until other explorers returned with similar stories of geysers and other geothermic activity.

There is dispute as to where Colter saw geysers. At the time, there were still active geysers in Wyoming. Colter's reports seemed to indicate that he saw them near the Stinking River.

The name refers to the high sulfur content in the water. That area is now Cody, Wyoming. The river has been renamed as the Shoshone River.

Historical marker of John Colter's birthplace,
Stuarts Draft, Virginia

When he was in his forties, he joined Nathan Boone's Rangers. Nathan Boone was the youngest son of the famous explorer, Daniel Boone. He took ill and died suddenly. The exact cause was never determined.

Of all of his feats of bravery, skill, and endurance during his life, one particular incident stands out. That, of course, is the Colter Run.

In 1808, John Colter and John Potts walked out of the Fort Raymond trading post in Montana and into the wilderness. They met up with friendly Flathead and Crow Indians. They convinced them to return with them to Fort Raymond for trading. On the way, they were attacked by Blackfeet. As many as 800 Indians were accompanying Colter and Potts, but the Blackfeet had twice that number. Despite the numerical advantage, the Blackfeet were forced to break off the attack and retreat. From that point on, the Blackfeet were sworn enemies of Colter and Potts.

The next year, 1809, Colter and Potts were set upon by the Blackfeet again. The two traders were canoeing up the Jefferson River, a tributary of the Missouri River in Montana. Several hundred natives appeared on the banks and ordered them to come ashore.

Colter waded ashore. He was stripped of his equipment and clothing. Potts refused to leave the canoe and was shot. Potts returned fire and then died in a hail of bullets. They brought his body ashore and hacked it to pieces.

Colter was not killed. He was told to wait. The Blackfeet had a council. They told him that they were letting him go. He asked for this clothes and equipment. They refused. He was to leave naked and with no guns, tools, or clothing.

Colter saw a group of young braves watching him intently. As he began to leave, he was told to run. He did not. He understood what was about to take place. Colter walked away at a normal pace, neither fast nor slow. He did not look back. He just slowly and deliberately walked away.

And then he heard a cry. He took his first look at the Blackfeet. The group of young braves was running at him. Colter broke into a run.

Colter's birth date is unknown, but he was between the ages of 33 and 40 at that time. Although a little old, he was in excellent physical shape and was naturally a swift runner. He soon outran all but one of the Indians.

He was tiring, and the gap between the two was closing. Colter fell. His nose smashed into a rock and began bleeding profusely. Blood poured down his face, neck and chest. He got up and ran.

The lead Blackfoot runner continued to close the distance between them. He carried a spear. Colter knew he would be caught soon. He suddenly turned and faced his pursuer. The brave was surprised. He awkwardly stumbled as he threw his spear. He threw it into the ground with such force that it shattered. Colter picked up the front half and killed the brave while he was still lying on the ground.

The other pursuers were well behind him, but coming fast. Colter took a blanket from the dead Indian and began running again. He was well ahead of the pack, but he couldn't lose them. They were good trackers. It was only a matter of time before they would catch him.

He reached the Madison River, a full five miles from the starting point of this death race. Colter was exhausted. He could not continue at this pace. They would soon catch him. He decided to take a big chance.

By the time the young braves arrived at the Madison River, Colter was nowhere to be seen. They found where he entered the river. They couldn't find where he exited. They milled around for a few minutes, and then they were off. They split up with the idea of finding his path and signaling to the others.

Colter's Hell on the Shoshone River near Cody, Wyoming

They never found him. Colter took the very risky option of hiding inside a beaver lodge. Beavers are very territorial. They will tear each other to pieces with their teeth and claws. They are the second-largest rodent in the world, and they can be vicious.

Colter hid quietly inside a lodge until nightfall. The beaver in the lodge did not attack him. Then he made his way to the closest outpost, naked and unarmed.

That is probably the most sensational version of this part of his story. Other accounts say he hid under a beaver dam, near a beaver dam, under a loose collection of logs, in an abandoned beaver lodge, etc.

Poster for the 1912 movie, John Colter's Escape

John Bradbury published Travels in the Interior of America a handful of years later which contained an account of Colter's Run. He described it as a "raft of drift timber" stuck up against the bank of the river. He said Colter dove below the raft and searched for spaces between the fallen trees where he could surface and breathe.

In any event, Colter did escape. The closest outpost was Lisa's Fort on the Bighorn. It took him a week. He was starving and suffering from exposure, but he was alive.

The next year, 1810, two of Colter's partners were killed by the Blackfeet. That was it for him. He packed up and returned to St. Louis. He left the wilderness forever, but his legend lives on.

BLACK BART

Black Bart was a hardworking soldier, miner, husband and father of four children. He was so upstanding that during the Civil War he earned the rank of First Sergeant and later both Second Lieutenant and First Lieutenant.

It took just one bad encounter to turn him into one of the most famous stagecoach robbers in American history. No one know what happened during that encounter, but what he did afterwards will be forever remembered.

Black Bart was born in 1829 as Charles Bolles in Norfolk, England. At the age of two, his father moved his family to Jefferson County, New York. In 1849, he traveled to California with two of his brothers, David and James. They had Gold Rush fever. They panned the North Fork of the American River near Sacramento.

They didn't have much luck, and all three of them returned to New York in 1852. Black Bart still had the Gold Rush fever. He went back to California with David, one of the brothers from the last trip, and Robert, a younger brother. James stayed home.

Charles Boles, Black Bart, the PO8 (poet)

Both of his brothers fell violently ill shortly after arrival in California. Neither one survived. He stayed and mined for two years, but eventually, he left California.

In 1854, according to his marriage certificate to Mary Elizabeth Johnson, he was now spelling his last name Boles with just one L. The happy couple had four children and lived in Decatur, Illinois.

When the Civil War rolled around, Black Bart enlisted in the 116th Illinois Regiment. It was a bloody war. Promotions were quick because of all the death. He enlisted as a private. Within a year, he was First Sergeant. Later he received commissions as a brevet officer. He rose to brevet first lieutenant. A brevet officer is a temporary rank awarded as needed. In the same way that we would say "acting mayor" or "acting police chief," he was called a brevet officer.

In any event, when the war was over, the often-promoted Black Bart returned to his wife and children in Illinois. He surely had a chest full of medals. He was wounded at the Battle of

Vicksburg. He fought in the Battle of Atlanta. He was part of Sherman's famous March to the Sea.

Despite all of his heroics, Black Bart remained plain old Charley Boles, loving husband and father. He was still a hardworking upstanding citizen, and he still had gold fever. This time he went to Idaho and Montana. He left in 1867. He never returned home again. In August 1871, his wife Mary received one final letter from him. In it, he told her of being treated badly by some employees of Wells Fargo. He vowed revenge. That was his last message to her. In time, she called herself Widow Boles and claimed he had died.

The incident with the Wells Fargo employees apparently had nothing to do with Wells Fargo. It was between Black Bart and his partner and two other men, either employees or protected by Wells Fargo. They wanted to buy his mine. Black Bart and his partner refused to sell. Somehow the two scorned buyers were able to shut off the water to the mine. That made it impossible to work the mine.

There isn't any information as to how Wells Fargo was involved in all of this. Your guess is as good as any. Perhaps they owned the water and were persuaded to shut it off. Perhaps it was shut off without permission. Perhaps, they bribed someone at Wells Fargo to shut it off. We'll never know.

In any event, mild-mannered, hardworking, war hero, Charley Boles was on the cusp of becoming Black Bart, Gentleman Bandit. He had just lost a mine that he thought would pay off big. He wanted revenge. He came up with a heck of a plan.

Somewhere, somehow, someplace, he stopped being Charley Boles and started being Charley Bolton with Black Bart as his stagecoach-robbing alter ego.

Charley Bolton was a well-dressed gentlemen, much more well-off than Charley Boles. The best guess is that he committed a few stagecoach robberies before he was rich enough to assume the Charley Bolton persona.

As to Black Bart, he signed two poems as Black Bart. He left them at the scenes of his third and fourth stagecoach robberies.

Before that time, if he was Black Bart, he was only Black Bart to himself.

At any rate, Charley Boles/Charley Bolton/Black Bart – whoever he was – robbed his first stagecoach on July 26, 1875. It was in Calaveras County, the locale of Mark Twain's story about his Celebrated Jumping Frog. It was a production worthy of Twain.

Down a narrow road came the stagecoach. Out of the bushes stepped a short thin man in a long coat (a duster). He carried a shotgun. A flour sack with two eye holes served as his mask. He topped off his outfit with a derby. He was always a gentleman.

The stagecoach came to a halt. "Please, throw down the box," he called out politely, but sternly. There were no guards on this stage. It was only John Shine, the driver, and a few passengers. He moved slow.

"If he dares to shoot, give him a solid volley, boys." Hearing this, Shine noticed rifles pointed at him from the surrounding bushes. He threw down the strongbox. A passenger offered Black Bart her purse. He refused. He told her that he was only interested in Wells Fargo property.

Black Bart forced open the strongbox and grabbed his loot. He warned the driver to stay on the stagecoach and disappeared into the bushes.

Shine, the driver, waited for the gang to follow. They didn't. In fact, they didn't move at all. Eventually, he dismounted the stage and examined the area. There was no gang. The rifles were carefully placed sticks.

It wasn't a particularly lucrative heist. The take was a mere $160. Future holdups would net much more. But he had successfully pulled off his first caper. And with that, the legend of Black Bart, Gentleman Bandit, was born.

You would think that a robbery like that could only be pulled off one time, but he did it again six months later. This time he held up a stage heading to Marysville, California. It was December 28, 1875. Black Bart was dressed the same way: duster coat, derby, and flour sack mask. His "gang" was in the bushes with their wooden rifles pointing at the stage.

Black Bart continued robbing stages until 1883. In total, he robbed 28 of them. Sometimes, especially in the beginning, he would go half a year or more between robberies. Other times, he committed several in quick succession. He robbed one on October 2, 1878, in Mendocino County, and then he robbed a second stage the next day. That stage was also on a run in Mendocino County.

Sometimes he would make a quip or share a joke with those he robbed. On the June 21, 1879, robbery, he said to the driver "Sure hope you have a lot of gold in that strongbox. I'm nearly out of money." On September 1, 1880, he said, "Hurry up the hounds. It gets lonesome in the mountains."

He was polite, and he was well-known for not harming anyone. Perhaps that was what prompted stage driver Horace Williams to ask Bart on October 8, 1881, "How much did you make?" Bart responded with "Not very much for the chances I take." He may have been telling the truth because he robbed another stage three days later.

"Graying brown hair, missing two of his front teeth, deep-set piercing blue eyes under heavy eyebrows. Slender hands and intellectual in conversation, well-flavored with polite jokes." Donna McCreary Eyewitness

What really set his reputation was his poetry. He left only two poems. After he robbed the stage to Duncan's Mills, California, on August 3, 1877, investigators found his first poem.

I've labored long and hard for bread
For honor and for riches
But on my corns too long you've tread
You fine-haired sons of bitches.

That's a bit risque for a man like Black Bart. Along with being polite, well-dressed, and dapper, he didn't swear when he robbed stagecoaches. Not once. Perhaps the poem was a result of his long-simmering hatred for Wells Fargo.

His next poem was left at the scene of his very next robbery. It was three stanzas. The poem at the previous robbery was the second stanza in this poem.

Here I lay me down to sleep
To await the coming morrow
Perhaps success, perhaps defeat
And everlasting sorrow

I've labored long and hard for bread
For honor and for riches
But on my corns too long you've tread
You fine-haired sons of bitches.

Let come what will, I'll try it on
My condition can't be worse
And if there's money in that box
'Tis money in my purse.

Each poem was signed the same way: Black Bart – The PO8. The "PO8" for the word "Poet" was another of his little jokes. After his second poem, he never again left a poem or a note. Since his poems were about robbing Wells Fargo stagecoaches, one can assume that his poetry was meant to state his position or hatred for Wells Fargo. And once stated, he didn't feel the need to expand on the subject.

Most stories about Black Bart say that he stole his name from a story published in the Sacramento Union newspaper. In The Case of Summerfield, William Henry Rhodes had a character named Black Bart that robbed Wells Fargo stagecoaches. It may also be that he heard of Black Bart, the famous pirate who captured over 400 ships.

After he was caught, Bart told investigators that the name just popped into his head. It could have been just that simple.

Bart was an unusual robber in more ways than his appearance and diction. Bart didn't ride horses. His getaways were on foot. As his notoriety rose, they put posses and agents on his trail immediately. He planned well. They never caught him leaving the scene of a robbery.

On his 28th and final robbery, Black Bart was shot in the hand. In his haste to escape, he lost a few personal belongings. Among them was a handkerchief with the laundry mark F. X. O. 7. The Wells Fargo agents scoured Sacramento looking for it, and they found it.

Ferguson & Bigg's California Laundry told investigators the name and address of Black Bart, and that was the end of his career. He was captured the same day. At first, he denied being Black Bart. He said he was T. Z. Spalding, a mining engineer. He kept up the charade for a while, but when the police found his real name in his Bible, he confessed to everything.

Even the police report on him makes note of his politeness and wit. It even added that he "eschews profanity." Wells Fargo only pressed charges on his last robbery. He was sentenced to six years. He served four and got out on good behavior.

Reporters surrounded him as he was released from prison. He was asked if he was going to rob any more stagecoaches. With a laugh, he said "No, gentlemen, I'm through with crime."

And when asked if he would write any more poetry, he responded with "Now didn't you hear me say that I am through with crime?"

Good ol' Black Bart. Always polite. Always the wit. A true PO8.

HENRY PLUMMER, OUTLAW SHERIFF

You can fool all of the people,
but not all of the time.

enry Plummer was a winner. Whatever he did was a success. Among other things that he did well, he was both an excellent sheriff and an outstanding outlaw. He died because he tried to be both at once.

William Henry Handy Plumer was born in 1832 in Maine. He moved west when he was 19, and by the age of 21, he was a successful gold miner and the owner of a ranch, a mine and a bakery in Nevada City, California, about 60 miles north of Sacramento. Somewhere along the way, he began spelling his name Plummer with two Ls.

Two years later, the town thought so much of him that they elected him both sheriff and city manager. He did well, and there was talk of him running for office on the state and national level.

He accomplished all of that by the age of 24. A year later, he killed a man and was sentenced to San Quentin for ten years. As a sheriff, he put Lucy Vedder under his protection from her husband. Plummer shot and killed John Vedder, the husband. He was tried, convicted, tried on appeal, and convicted again.

Henry Plummer, Sheriff of Bannack, Montana

It was a second-degree murder conviction. He must have been doing something other than simply protecting Lucy Vedder. Whatever it was that he did, the juries thought he deserved prison time.

Some say he was having an affair with Lucy Vedder. Some say he engaged in a duel with her husband. Another version is that he was helping Mrs. Vedder to pack, and the husband came home drunk and pulled a gun on the sheriff. Still another one says Mrs. Vedder and Plummer took up adjoining rooms in a hotel as their love nest.

All we know is the sheriff shot and killed Mr. Vedder, and the jury did not believe his claims of self defense. So it was off to San Quentin with Sheriff Plummer. He was sentenced to ten years.

This didn't sit well with a lot of the town's citizens. He was still popular in Nevada City. His supporters wrote to the governor begging for a pardon. And son-of-a-gun, he got one. He was released after serving only two years. The governor noted Plummer's tuberculosis as a reason for a humanitarian release.

That was his first killing. There were more. He always had a reason. It was never a reason that explained everything satisfactorily, but it always kept him out of jail. Somehow.

His next killing was a man named William "Buckskin Bill" Riley. He was the second San Quentin escaped prisoner that he tried to capture. The first was Ten-Year Smith. There isn't much written about his capture, but apparently Ten-Year stabbed Plummer or threw a knife at him. Either way, Plummer was injured, but still held onto Ten-Year until help arrived.

Riley also fought against capture. Plummer killed him. Then he went to the police with the body. After investigating, the police determined that Plummer acted in self defense and within the law. Reportedly, as he was released, the police advised him to leave California.

Plummer decided the Washington Territory was his destination. It would be the scene of his third killing. This one might not have been his fault, although by all accounts, it appears that he started the trouble that caused the killing. In any event, he was soon in the mining town of Florence which is now part of Idaho.

Pat Ford disliked Plummer and his friends. Ford owned a dance hall, which possibly had a brothel in it. He ordered them to leave for being loud and unruly. Plummer had two of his friends with him at the time. They went outside to their horses and were preparing to leave. Suddenly, Ford steps outside with a gun in each hand and starts firing.

The story says that Ford fired eleven shots. None of them struck Plummer. His friend, Charles Ridgley, was shot twice in the leg. Plummer's horse was seriously injured and had to be destroyed. Plummer and his two friends opened fire and killed Ford in a volley of bullets.

He would have been lynched, but he skedaddled faster than Ford's friends pursued. Later when everybody calmed down, Plummer was perceived a lot more sympathetically. He was long gone by that time, but I guess it was nice to know that they didn't want to string him up anymore.

The next guy he killed was a friend named Jack Cleveland. Plummer and Cleveland fell in love with the same woman, Electra Bryan. Plummer and Electra became engaged. It caused a great deal of animosity between the two men.

One January night in 1863 in a saloon in Bannack, Montana, Cleveland goaded Plummer into a fight. Plummer reportedly tried to discourage a fight by firing a shot into the ceiling, but Cleveland would not back down. Cleveland drew his gun. Plummer shot him down.

That's the story, but Plummer was charged with murder once again. And once again, they found him innocent. This time, it was a miner's court and jury. The jury members, and possibly the judge, were friends with Plummer. There wasn't much chance that he would be convicted. It might have been a different story if they had an actual judge and jury, but in those days, before the law officially came to town, the miners, ranchers, etc., had to deal with matters their own way.

Instead of a conviction, he was acquitted. A few months later in May 1863, the citizens of Bannack voted him in as sheriff. In August 1863, he was astonishingly appointed Deputy US Marshal for the surrounding territory. It did not work out the way that they thought it would. Crime rose dramatically during his time as sheriff. It wasn't long before the citizens of Bannack, Virginia City, Nevada City and the Alder Gulch area were up in arms, and pointing fingers at everybody.

Plummer organized a gang. They called themselves the Innocents. Eventually, they had about 100 men. It was so large that they used a secret handshake and a signal to indicate they were part of the gang. These men worked for themselves as often as for the gang itself. The attraction, of course, was that they were protected by Plummer, the very man who was supposed to be arresting them.

Usually, the murders were part of the robberies, but sometimes they were for revenge or for no discernible reason. Citizens were warned not to talk. Some were killed to prevent them from talking. At least one man was killed immediately after reporting a crime to Plummer.

The major trouble began in October of that year. On the 13th of that month, businessman Lloyd Magruder and four men were murdered for his gold, estimated at $12,000. On October 26, a stage was robbed, netting $2,800 for the bandits. Incidents like this happened very frequently in the final months of 1863.

Estimates are that over 100 citizens were murdered in the last quarter of 1863 and the very beginning of 1864. The first step toward peace was the December 1863 trial of George Ives. This was another miners' court, but the miners on this jury were tired of the murders and robberies. They found him guilty, and he was hanged on December 21, 1863.

Two days after the trial, the miners of the nearby towns created The Vigilance Committee of Alder Gulch. It was formed in response to all the criminal activity. In its first two months of existence, the Committee captured and hung up to two dozen men.

On January 4, 1864, the vigilantes captured and hung two men: Erastus Red Yeager (sometimes Yager) and George Brown. They told the two men that they were taking them to town to stand trial. Yeager broke down and told all he knew. He named dozens of men, and he fingered Plummer as the leader. The posse promptly hanged both men.

One of the men in that posse was Captain James Williams. He had investigated at least one of the prior murders. He probably had heard of a previous incident involving a teenager named Henry Tilden and three highwaymen. They attempted to rob him, but he had no money. Tilden was told he could go, but he was warned to say nothing. When he got to town, he identified Sheriff Plummer as one of the outlaws.

Less than a week later, more than 50 men came for Sheriff Plummer, Deputy Buck Stinson and Deputy Ned Ray. They were marched into town and taken to the same gallows run by Plummer. Stinson and Ray were hanged first. On the gallows with a rope around his neck, Sheriff Plummer, head of the gang of Innocents, told the vigilantes that he would lead them to $100,000 in stolen gold. They declined the offer. He was hanged next to his two deputies.

The vigilantes went on to hang as many gang members as

they could find. They visited nearby towns, rooted them out, and summarily executed them. One can only imagine that some of the accused were innocent. They didn't get a trial. There was very little time between arrest and hanging. The vigilantes were in no mood to listen.

They didn't kill every man they captured. They released two young outlaws. They sent one to Bannack and one to Lewiston with orders to tell the rest of the gang to move out of the territory. The widespread murders and robberies were over. Things rapidly returned to normal.

Despite Erasmus Red's confession, Henry Tilden's identification, the general consensus that Plummer was a gang leader, and the immediate cessation of crime after the death of Plummer, some modern historians are attempting to prove Plummer innocent.

For one thing, they discount Erasmus Red's confession. Instead, they cast doubt on the posse. If the posse made up the story about the confession, that would throw doubt upon the guilt of Plummer.

The vigilantes might have been the real criminals. They might have strung up Plummer so they would have a free hand to do their holdups.

Perhaps. Perhaps not. We'll never know for sure.

But crime rapidly returned to normal after Plummer had his necktie party.

HUGH GLASS AND THE GRIZZLY ATTACK

They said he was dead. He didn't stay dead.

The story of Hugh Glass is undoubtedly true. However, the story has been amply embellished through the ages. Hugh Glass did not write or dictate his memoirs. The story of his grizzly bear attack appeared in newspapers two years after it occurred. Glass didn't write or contribute to the article. The author apparently wrote it as literary fiction based on fact.

How much is fact? We know that the story is essentially true. Glass was attacked by a bear. He was almost killed. His friends left him for dead. Injured and without weapons he walked and crawled 200 miles to civilization.

Pretty much everything else about the story could be the result of a sloppy historian's daydream. For instance, the popular version of the story says Jim Bridger played a role. Some say it was a different man named Bridges.

Illustration of Hugh Glass and the bear attack;
Artist unknown

We will never know the full truth. The Old West is full of mysteries that will never be solved. This is one of them. Here is what we know. Or what we think we know.

Hugh Glass was born in 1783 in Pennsylvania near Philadelphia. Possibly in Scranton. The next thing we know about him is that he might have been a pirate in his 30s. Glass said he was captured by Jean Lafitte off the coast of Texas in 1816. He served on the pirate ship for two years. At the end, he was fearful for his life and jumped ship with a fellow sailor. They both made it to shore near what is now Galveston, Texas. They had no maps, no weapons, no knowledge of the area. They wandered for a whopping 1,000 miles through territory owned by Karankawas, Osage, Comanche, and Kiowa tribes. Through amazing luck, they didn't meet any Indians. If they had, they would likely have been killed.

They did, however, meet up with a band of Skidi or Wolf Pawnee. This tribe was known for a ritualistic human sacrifice called the Morning Star Ceremony. In short detail, the ceremony was intended to ensure good crops, health, and a bountiful life.

Glass's fellow escaped pirate was chosen to be first. Details will not be given here. Explanations of the ritual can be accessed on the Internet if one so chooses. Suffice it to say that the man died.

Glass was next. When they came for him, Glass produced a "large package of vermilion." The broad definition of "vermilion" is simply a red pigment. The chief was impressed with the gift, halted the ceremony, and adopted Glass as his son. Like much of Glass's story, this incident cannot be verified, and it appears to be false. A man wandering in the wilderness like Glass would have use for a great many things, but a large package of vermilion would not be one of them. It would be an unnecessary burden.

At any rate, Glass was said to live with the Indians for several years. During his time with the Skidi, he mastered how to survive in the wilderness. He married a young Wolf Pawnee.

It is sometimes reported that in 1821 Glass traveled to St. Louis with a delegation of Pawnees for a meeting with authorities. Maybe so; maybe not. We do know for certain that the next year, General William Henry Ashley organized an expedition to explore the Missouri River. Many of the volunteers would later earn reputations as explorers and mountain men. Among them were William Sublette, Jim Bridger and Jedediah Smith. The expedition was known as Ashley's Hundred. Glass was not a part of the original venture, but he joined them in 1823.

That same year, the expedition was attacked by the Arikara tribe near what is now Mobridge, South Dakota. Fourteen died. Ten were wounded, including Glass who sustained a leg injury. One of the dead was John S. Gardner. He sent a letter to Gardner's father. Glass was known to be illiterate. He must have dictated it to one of the expedition members. Today, the letter is in the possession of the South Dakota State Historical Society. It is one of the few pieces of hard evidence about Glass's life, despite it not being written by him.

> *Dr Sir: My painfull duty it is to tell you of the deth of yr son wh befell at the hands of the Indians 2d June in the early morning. He died a little while after he was*

shot and asked me to inform you of his sad fate.

We brought him to the ship when he soon died. Mr. Smith a young man of our company made a powerful prayr wh moved us all greatly and I am persuaded John died in peace. His body we buried with others near this camp and marked the grave with a log. His things we will send to you. The savages are greatly treacherous.

We traded with them as friends but after a great storm of rain and thunder they came at us before light and many were hurt. I myself was shot in the leg. Master Ashley is bound to stay in these parts till the traitors are rightly punished. Yr Obt Svt Hugh Glass

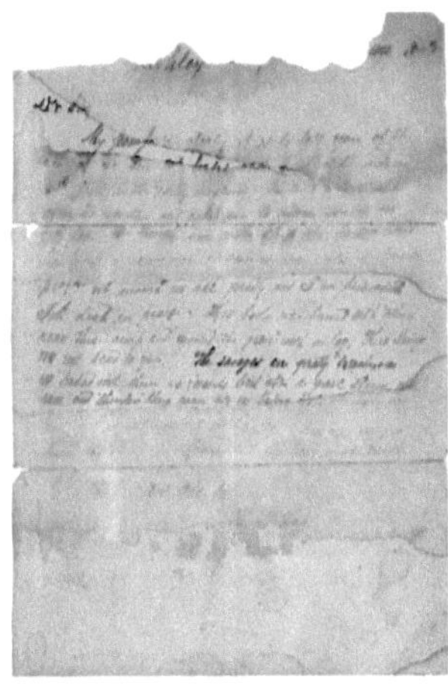

Hugh Glass letter on display in South Dakota

Ashley's plan was to haul keelboats up the river. A keelboat is a raft's rich cousin. It has a flat bottom so it can navigate shallow water. The inside is mostly an open area so freight can be easily loaded and unloaded. The better ones had a roof or another method of sheltering the goods from the rain and elements. Ashley wanted to pack them with hides and goods, and then float them back down to civilization for sale. The Arikara fight convinced him to change his plans.

After that, he took his boats only as far up the river as they could safely travel. From there, trappers and hunters set out on foot. By breaking the reliance on the river, this greatly widened the area that they could trap and hunt.

His alterations led to what became known as the Rocky Mountain Rendezvous where trappers and hunters would gather to sell their wares. In the spring, traders would haul in supplies for the trappers and hunters. In the fall, trappers would bring in their pelts.

"Mirth, songs, dancing, shouting, trading, running, jumping, singing, racing, target-shooting, yarns, frolic, with all sorts of extravagances that white men or Indians could invent." James Beckwourth

To this day, the yearly rendezvous continues. It is mostly for tourists, but it keeps the spirit of the mountain man alive. Muzzle-loaded rifle contests, tomahawk throwing, archery, dancing, singing, and tall tales are staples at these gatherings.

Glass was in one of the first parties to set out overland. This party was led by Andrew Henry, the partner of General Ashley. Their destination was the Yellowstone River. Glass hunted for the party. As such, he was far out in front of the main group. He could expect no immediate help if he ran into trouble. For an experienced woodsman, he made a serious mistake. He got between a mother bear and her cubs.

In an instant, the mother charged. She completely mauled him before Glass was able to kill the bear. Glass suffered gashes and slashes over most of his body. His scalp was half ripped off. His throat was punctured and slashed. One leg was broken.

The party was a long way from civilization. They had no doctor. Carrying Glass with them further into the wilderness would not have helped Glass. It might have ensured his death.

Volunteers were asked for. An $80 bonus was offered. Two stepped forward: John Fitzgerald and Jim Bridger (or someone named Bridges). If Glass survived, they were to bring him along to the main party. If he died, they were to bury him.

The two men should be given credit for volunteering to stay with him. It was Arikara territory, and if caught, they would be summarily killed. They stayed with Glass, but they never expected him to live. They dug his grave on the first day. Glass, however, refused to die.

He was still alive, but not conscious, on the fifth day after the main group departed. The two men feared they would be caught by the Indians. They took his gun, knife, flint, and belongings. Then they headed off to find Henry and the main party.

Whether they buried him, left him there, or moved him to a spot near a spring, history doesn't say with certainty. We do know that they left the unconscious Glass alone, unarmed, and without any of the tools a mountain man would need.

The two men reported that Glass died and was buried. They said that they were set upon by the Arikara while burying him. Their lies would come back to haunt them. Unknown to them, Glass had regained consciousness. He was almost mortally wounded. His leg had not been set, nor were his wounds tended to. He did it himself. Despite a broken leg, deep slashes to his face, head, chest, and assorted other injuries, he began crawling to a small trading post, Fort Kiowa on the Missouri River.

The exact route that he traveled is unknown, but it is clear that it was at least 200 miles. Some estimate it to be considerably more than that.

On the trip, his wounds became infected. Glass knew about gangrene and how to deal with it from the Indians. Maggots were the key. He allowed them to eat the infected flesh. It sounds horrible, but it likely saved his life.

There is a story that Glass woke up one day to find a grizzly bear licking his wounds clean. One version says the bear was eating the maggots out of the wounds. This is extremely unlikely. Most likely, it is just another embellishment to his fantastic story.

He didn't have a gun or even a knife. Food was hard to come by. At first, because he was crawling, he was lucky if he could find berries. Most likely, he ate insects, worms, and the leaves or roots of any edible plants he found. One story says he ran across a buffalo carcass and ate what the wolves had left. Another says he ran into a pack of wolves devouring a buffalo calf. In that story, he was able to steal away with half the buffalo after the wolves had their fill. He found a good place to hide and ate for days.

If you are ever in South Dakota, make sure to visit Thunder Butte in Ziebach County. It towers over the plains and can be seen for miles. The Lakotas call it Wakinyan Paha. In traditional lore, the Lakotas believe thunder originates on the butte. They use the butte as an easy navigation aide. Glass used it too. It may have saved his life.

Thunder Butte, South Dakota

Eventually, he reached the Missouri River. He either made a crude raft or he was given a small hide boat by friendly Lakota Indians. Then he floated down the river to Fort Kiowa and civilization. When he arrived, he rested until he had recovered sufficiently to travel. Then he set out to find the men who had deserted him.

First thing he did was travel to Fort Henry, but all he found was a note saying that Andrew Henry took his men to a new frontier outpost. It was on the Bighorn River. This fort was also known as Fort Henry.

It was at this new fort that he came upon Bridger (Bridges). He was very young and inexperienced at the time. Glass forgave him. He decided that the adult Fitzgerald was more responsible than the teenage Bridger.

Glass joined up with the Ashley Hundred again at Fort Henry. He remained there a while due to severe weather. He would have stayed all winter, but Henry needed to send a message to Fort Atkinson, a U. S. Army post in Nebraska.

Hugh Glass sculpture in Lemmon, South Dakota,
by John Lee Lopez

Glass volunteered to be one of five men to make the trip. Henry was offering extra pay due to the weather and the hostile Indians that they might encounter. Glass didn't care about the money or the hazards. He had heard that Fitzgerald had enlisted in the Army and was stationed at Fort Atkinson.

The men set off for Fort Atkinson. One story says the five men were attacked by the Arikara. Two men were killed. Two got away together. Glass escaped also, but without his weapon. The other two thought he was killed. They continued their journey without him.

Glass had some of his equipment. He walked overland to Fort Atkinson.

In any event, Hugh Glass walked into Fort Atkinson in June 1824. He found Fitzgerald and wanted to fight. An officer intervened and warned Glass that killing Fitzgerald would make Glass a criminal. The officer forced Fitzgerald to give Glass his gun. Glass was admonished to leave Fitzgerald alone or face the wrath of the U. S. Army. For his part, Glass told Fitzgerald that he would kill him the day he became a civilian.

Glass continued to have adventures working for the Ashley Hundred and working for himself as a free trapper. He had a close call with the Shoshones once. He was struck in the back by an arrow. The point lodged in his spine. A fellow trapper operated on him with a straight razor, and he recovered.

In the late winter of 1833, the Arikara ambushed Glass and two other men, Hilain Menard and Edward Colin Rose. The attack was on the Yellowstone River. All three were killed.

"They scalped them and left part of the Scalps
of each tied to poles on the grounds of the
murder." John F. A. Sanford, Indian Agent

And that was the end of Hugh Glass, mountain man, explorer, American hero.

BISBEE MASSACRE

*Four murdered; five
hanged; one lynched*

Bisbee, Arizona was the scene of a bumbling robbery that turned into an awful bloodbath that killed four people, one of them a pregnant woman. The story is one of greed. Nothing more; nothing less.

John Heath led a fairly disreputable life. He was suspected of everything from pimping to burglary to rustling. He even had a couple of stickups to his credit. He was a deputy sheriff of Cochise County, Arizona for a short time, but that didn't seem to affect his outlaw ways before, during, or after his time as a lawman.

Heath was a smart man. He organized a gang to steal the payroll for the Copper Queen Mine. The mine was a large operation. Bisbee was a small town in Cochise County. Tombstone was the county seat. Bisbee didn't have a bank. The mine's monthly payroll was stored in the safest place around: the Goldwater and Castaneda Mercantile. They had a safe. It was the only one in the area.

Every month the Copper Queen Mine would have around $7,000 brought in to pay their miners. That's about $200,000 in today's money. The whole town knew when the money was coming in. Payday was the 10th. The money came in a day or two before that.

Tombstone of the First Five Men to be "Legally Hanged" in Tombstone.

Heath came up with a plan. He gathered five of his no-account friends. They were to rob the store and the safe. While they did the dirty work, Heath was to keep himself in plain view of the town's citizens. He knew he would be the first person suspected. On the day of the robbery, he and a man named Nathan Waite were busy working on their dance hall.

Some say the day of the robbery was the first day the hall was open for business. Others say the dance hall had been open for some time, and that was where Heath became friends with some of his outlaw buddies.

In any event, Heath innocently went about his business while his five friends robbed the store. The five men were Billy Delaney, James "Tex" Howard, Daniel "York" Kelly, Omer "Red" Sample, and Big Dan Dowd. They had a simple plan: rob the store; steal the payroll; ride away.

It wasn't a good plan. It worked, but it really wasn't a success. Four of the men wore masks. Tex Howard did not. All five were known in the town. Howard just didn't care if he was identified.

Howard and one or two of the other men entered the store. The others acted as lookouts standing on the front steps. They forced the store owner to open the safe. To their surprise, it did not contain the payroll. It had not yet arrived. It was still on the road several dozen miles away.

This is where their greed got to them. They took what was in the safe. They robbed the customers and employees in the store. They took their time and robbed a few customers who wandered by. Their greed kept them from leaving immediately, and it proved their downfall.

Eventually, the town's citizens became suspicious. They noticed the armed men standing out in front of the store. They may have observed that customers went in the store but did not come out. In any event, the town became suspicious, and the men standing guard outside knew it. They became anxious waiting for their cohorts.

The first death was J. C. Tappenier. He walked outside the Bon Ton Saloon and stared at them. They ordered him back inside. He refused, and they shot him dead with a bullet to his head.

The next was Deputy Sheriff Tom Smith. He left his wife in the restaurant across the street and ordered the men to drop their weapons. After identifying himself as a lawman, one of the men said, "Then you are the one we want." He was the second one to die.

A stray bullet hit a man named Indian Joe in the leg. The owner of the Bisbee House restaurant, Mrs. Annie Roberts, was the victim of another stray bullet. She was standing in the front doorway when a bullet fatally struck her. She was pregnant at the time. She died a few hours later. A driver for a freight company was caught in the crossfire and shot in the chest. He died later that night.

All of the shooting happened very quickly. The men inside heard it begin. Before they exited the building, it was over. All five mounted their horses and rode out of town. Deputy Sheriff Billy Daniels emptied his revolvers at them as they raced away, but he missed hitting anyone.

No one knows exactly how much they were able to steal. Some say it was less than $1,000. Other estimates put it as much as $3,000. At any rate, it was a good haul for a quick robbery, but it wasn't close to the $7,000 that they expected.

Once they were safely out of town, they stopped at a place known as Soldier's Hole and divided up the money. Then they split up. That made it a little harder to track them down, but since one of the robbers, Tex Howard, did not wear a mask, they had their suspicions immediately as to who the other bandits were.

But they surely didn't know everything. One of the first things that was done was to organize two posses. One of them contained John Heath, the man who planned the robbery, and Nathan Waite, a friend and business partner of John Heath.

At the subsequent trial of John Heath, Deputy Daniels testified that Heath tried to mislead the posse by saying that the trail split up. Heath maintained that two men split off from the original group of five. If Heath was telling the truth, it would be the greatest proof of his innocence since he would have no incentive to capture the outlaws if he was the actual leader of the gang.

As it turned out, the outlaws did split up with two of them going their own way. Both posses lost the trail, and no one was captured immediately. It wouldn't take long before all of them were in jail, mainly because of their stupidity.

Tex Howard was the man who didn't wear a mask; so he was identified on sight during the robbery. The rest of the men were assumed to be his friends.

The first man captured was York Kelly. He was captured near Deming, New Mexico. Tex Howard and Red Sample were caught because they went to Clifton, Arizona, where they were known. A bartender notified the law. A posse was assembled. They were quickly brought in.

That left Big Dan Dowd and Billy Delaney as the remaining outlaws on the run. They went to Mexico. Deputy Daniels crossed the border and captured both of them. Dowd was apprehended in Los Corralitos, Sonora. Delaney had gotten into a fight in Minas Prietas and was in a Mexican jail.

A large part of the reason why the outlaws were quickly captured was that the mining company offered a large reward. Deputy Daniels traded one share of the reward with the Mexican authorities for Delaney's release.

The robbery occurred on December 8, 1883. On February 6, 1884, they were indicted. Trial began on February 17, and a few days later, all five were convicted and sentenced to hang.

Heath was not part of that trial. He had a separate trial where he admitted to planning the robbery. He vehemently denied any responsibility for the murders though. He was sentenced to life in the Yuma prison. The townspeople were not happy with that verdict. They felt that he should be strung up with the rest of the gang. They weren't about to let him be carted off to the relative safety of the Yuma Territorial Prison.

Heath's trial began on February 20, 1884. He was convicted and sentenced to life on February 21. Fifty or more armed miners broke into the nearby Tombstone jail on February 22 and drug Heath into the street. They had their own idea of justice.

At the corner of First and Toughnut Streets, they threw a rope over a telegraph pole. Before they dragged him upward, Heath was reported to have asked that they not mutilate or shoot his body after hanging. And with that, they pulled him into the air where he strangled to death.

Afterwards, someone placed a sign on the telegraph pole with the following message:

JOHN HEITH
Was hanged to this pole by the
CITIZENS OF COCHISE COUNTY
For participating in the Bisbee massacre
As a proved accessory
At 8:00 a.m., February 22, 1884
(Washington's Birthday)
ADVANCE ARIZONA!

John Heath, February 22, 1884

Dr. George Goodfellow witnessed the hanging of John Heath. He was the County Coroner. It was his job to attend hangings and testify to the time of death. He later convened a coroner's jury, and they released this statement:

> *"We the undersigned, a jury of inquest, find that John Heath came to his death from emphysema of the lungs–a disease common in high altitudes–which might have been caused by strangulation, self-inflicted or otherwise."*

The other five men had been left in their cells when Heath was dragged outside. The townspeople were not concerned about them. They were scheduled to be hanged on March 28, and the citizens were content to let the law handle their deaths.

On the appointed day, the town of Bisbee was filled to overflowing with sightseers and tourists. Over 1,000 people attended the hangings. The bars and dance halls did steady business. It has been described as a circus or carnival atmosphere.

John Heath's grave in Tombstone, Arizona

John Heath has a tombstone in the Boothill Graveyard in Tombstone, but he was moved to his hometown of Terrell, Texas, and buried in an unmarked grave.

His five outlaw friends remain in Boothill. They are known as the first men in Tombstone to be legally hanged.

LIVER-EATING
JOHNSON

*A Man with a Long Memory
and a Short Temper*

The mountain man known as Jeremiah Johnson (in the movies) or as Liver-Eating Johnson (to historians) cut a wide swath through the Rocky Mountains in the late 1800s. He was an experienced hunter, trapper, soldier, sailor, lawman, guide, miner, etc. If it was a manual labor job, he probably did it sometime in his life.

However, he wouldn't be well remembered except for one thing: The man really knew how to hold a grudge.

Most details about Johnson are up for interpretation, especially his earlier years. His exploits are clouded by tall tales and embellishments.

Most stories say that he came from back East, probably New Jersey, probably born in 1824, and his name at the time was probably John Garrison. Probably. About the age of 22 or so, he joined the US Navy during the Mexican-American War. He was a bad fit with the strict military discipline of the Navy. One day, he struck an officer and jumped ship ending his sailing career.

At this point, he changed his name to John Johnston (or

Johnson) and headed west to try his luck at the gold strikes in Montana. He doesn't seem to have been a success as he took to supplying steamboats with cut wood. This was called wood-hawking. Johnson would cut wood on a riverbank and leave a sign for the riverboats. When they picked up the wood, they would leave payment for him to find the next time he wandered by.

Johnson has been described as a virtual bear of a man standing over 6 feet and weighing 260 pounds of lean muscle. He would have been an imposing man in any setting.

Somewhere along the way, he ran into the Flathead Indians and married a woman named Swan. They lived happily until Swan was killed by a young Crow brave on a hunting trip. No explanation is given, but one can assume that it was an accident since she was killed by a hunting party and not a war party.

Nonetheless, Johnson vowed revenge, not on the individual Crow hunter, but on the whole tribe. He began a vendetta and hunted down and killed Crows by the dozens. Some estimate that he killed as many as 300. That is an astronomical claim, and like many of the tales about Johnson, it is also most likely false.

Johnson was reputed to eat the livers of those he killed. He did so to interfere with their happiness in the afterlife. The Crow believed that the liver was important, and removing it was an insult to their way of life. Eating the liver was gruesome and just added to their hatred of Johnson.

And so if the legends are to be believed Johnson embarked on a 25-year mission of killing Crow braves. If he really did kill 300, then he had to average one man per month for those 25 years. Here is where the liver-eating story ends. After more than two dozen years of relentless stalking and killing, he made friends with the Crow, called them his brothers, and moved on to his next adventure.

Johnson's cabin in Red Lodge, Montana

This is an example of another great Old West tale with very little authentication. The more likely story is one that is much less bloody and thousands of times less interesting.

During a battle with the Sioux, Johnson made a small offhand joke about eating liver. It had nothing to do with the Crow, his wife, a vendetta, or dozens and dozens of bodies. It was just a joke.

From that inconsequential remark grew his reputation and his nickname. The tales grew larger and larger as it evolved over the years. Here is one example of how outrageous the claims became.

During his 25-year rampage, Johnson was captured by a party of Blackfeet. They had nothing against Johnson, but they planned to sell him to his mortal enemies, the Crow. Johnson, sneaky son-of-a-gun that he was, managed to break his bonds, kill the only guard, and escape.

Wait. That's not quite the whole story. According to legend, after he killed the guard, he sawed off the man's leg with his knife, and then he took the leg with him when he left.

No, that's not quite the whole story either. He took the leg and used it as a club to fight his way out of the camp. That's the whole story.

No, it isn't. The whole story is that he then munched on the leg as he made his way through the wilderness to safety. Yes, somebody somewhere embellished the story so much that he became a cannibal. Well, more of a cannibal. He had to be a cannibal if he was eating all of those livers.

That story is outrageous. If he did manage to overcome his captor, he wouldn't have waited around to cut off the man's leg. He would have skedaddled quick like the proverbial bunny. Sawing off a leg would take a great deal of time. If he had been caught in the middle of such a gruesome operation, he would have been instantly killed.

It is up to you to believe or disbelieve the liver-eating aspect of his story. This author votes a resounding no. There doesn't appear to be any positive evidence for it.

Most of what we truly know about Johnson comes from government records. We know he was in the Navy during the Mexican-American War of 1846/48. We know that he was a Union soldier in 1864/65. We know that 20 years later he was a constable in Coulson, Montana, around 1882, and he was a town marshal in Red Lodge, Montana, about ten years after that.

About the only other evidence that we definitely know about him is that he died in Santa Monica, California, on January 21, 1900.

Liver-Eating Johnson's Grave in Cody, Wyoming

Johnson was obviously a very capable mountain man. He spent a good deal of his life living off the land, exploring, trading, fighting, and generally living a hell-for-leather life of hardship and independence.

Did he deserve his liver-eating nickname? Was it all the result of tall tall tales around the campfires? No one can say with certainty, but the evidence definitely points to good story telling rather than accurate reporting.

THE SANDBAR FIGHT WITH JIM BOWIE

Jim Bowie was one of the heroes of the Alamo. Besides that, he was the inventor of the Bowie knife, and he was a renowned knife fighter. All of that is true. He was one of the real heroes of the Alamo. He did work with various blacksmiths and metal workers to design the knife that bears his name. And he was well known as a knife fighter.

The only problem with that last statement is that there is only one verifiable instance of him ever fighting with a knife. That happened during the Sandbar Fight, and Jim got his butt handed to him on a platter. He almost died. Despite having five doctors on hand, he was lucky to survive.

The incident leading to his injuries is known as the Sandbar Fight, but it could easily have been called the Sandbar Duel. It was one of the most gentlemenly of duels. Rules were followed. The duelists were well-mannered and polite. At the end, they shook hands and both walked away unharmed.

Then all bloody hell broke loose.

Jim Bowie

On September 19, 1827, two opposing groups met on a sandbar outside of Natchez, Mississippi. They were there for a duel between two local business leaders: Dr. Thomas H. Maddox and Samuel L. Wells III. They both lived in Alexandria, Louisiana, but they chose this sandbar location to avoid interference from local sheriffs. There were strong laws against dueling in Louisiana.

The opponents had a laundry list of grievances against each other, involving money, election fixing, the honor of a woman, and general dislike for each other and their supporters.

The two men were leaders in their town. Each one had their followers. Some of them were quite violent. Jim Bowie had been shot previously by one of the spectators, a man named Norris Wright. Bowie had to be pulled off the man, or he likely would have beaten him to death.

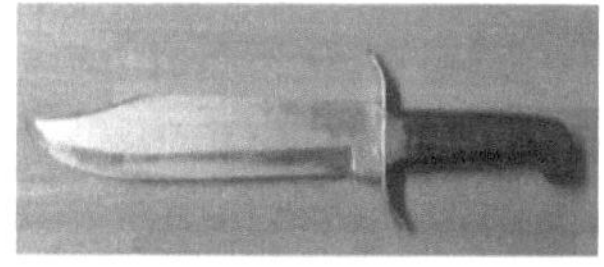

A Bowie knife

The two duelists were determined to act like gentlemen during the duel, and they did. Each of them was accompanied by their seconds and their personal physicians.

Samuel Wells brought Major George McWorther as his second and Dr. Richard Cuny as his physician. Dr. Maddox had Colonel Robert Crain as his second and Dr. James Denny as his physician. Besides those six people, each side had supporters of approximately equal numbers. Seventeen or more people were on the sandbar that day to observe or participate in the duel.

By all accounts, the duel followed formal rules, and all participants acted honorably. Just like you see on television or in movies, each man stood bravely facing the other with one bullet apiece. They both fired, and they both missed.

A short break was taken. Their weapons were reloaded, and they once again faced each other on the field of honor. Again, they both fired, and again, they both missed.

Wells and Maddox, both happy to be alive and unharmed, declared the duel to be over and shook hands.

What happened in the next few minutes can only be told in general terms. Everybody on that sandbar were soon involved in a deadly shootout or running from said shootout.

The most common scenario has the participants on both sides (duelists, seconds, and physicians) concluding the duel and then approaching the spectators who supported Maddox. Before they reached them, they were intercepted by the supporters of Wells.

General Cuny, a Wells supporter, was heard to call out to Colonel Crain, who was Dr. Maddox's second. "Colonel Crain, this is a good time to settle our difficulty."

Crain was armed with two pistols. He fired at Cuny, but missed. Bowie was hit with the stray shot and fell to the ground. Crain and Cuny fired upon each other until Cuny fell mortally wounded.

Bowie, although injured, rose to his feet and attacked Crain with his knife. Crain's weapons were now empty. He struck Bowie with the butt of one of the guns, driving Bowie to the ground for the second time.

Nathan Wright, Bowie's enemy from before, shot at Bowie as he lay on the ground. He missed. Then he unsheathed his cane sword and stabbed at Bowie, striking him in the chest, but not penetrating past the bone.

Bowie, while still lying wounded and dazed on the ground, reached up and grabbed Wright by the neck and pulled him down upon his knife.

As he tried to rise, Bowie was shot again and stabbed again. There were more shots. Bowie was hit in the arm. He stabbed one man. Another ran upon seeing the first man bleeding.

"Bowie at the same time was drawing his pistol. I drew away at him; he says now that I did not touch him but drew his fire. He lies; I shot him through the body as he is shot. I could not miss, shooting not further than ten feet and the object is to excuse his conduct for killing our poor friend [Major Wright]." Colonel Robert Crain

Bowie wasn't the only man injured in this all-out fight, but he certainly was the most injured survivor. Five of the seventeen people at the duel were doctors. Bowie was lucky to receive such prompt attention. One physician was heard to say "How he lived is a mystery to me, but live he did."

Samuel Cuny was killed by Colonel Crain. Norris Wright was killed by Jim Bowie. Alfred Blanchard was badly injured, partly by Jim Bowie. Dr. Denny was shot twice, but not fatally. Crain was barely grazed by a bullet.

"Colonel Crain, I do not think, under the circumstances, you ought to have shot me." Jim Bowie

Curiously, Wells and Maddox, the two duelists, escaped un-scathed by the duel and by the ensuing fight. They went on to attack each other and their supporters in court and in the press.

Nothing much came from it though. Wells took sick and died a few months later. A Mississippi Grand Jury examined the matter, but no indictments or arrests were made.

Bowie's fame grew as this story was told through the decades following. He faced armed men with only his knife. He was struck by bullets multiple times. He was knocked down multiple times. But he never quit. He rose time and again and attacked his opponents, killing one, and injuring several.

Bowie's injury total for the Sandbar Fight is impressive. He was shot two or three times. He was stabbed or slashed up to seven times. He received a severe blow to the head from Colonel Crain.

By the time he rode into the Alamo, he was known throughout Texas and the West as an experienced knife fighter. This one fight, though, on this isolated sandbar was the only known instance of Bowie involved in a fight with a knife.

That was it. One fight, one time, and it made him famous. And it should have. It was a hell of a fight.

THE SILKS-FULTON NUDE DUEL

A Little Sex Never Hurt Anyone.
Or Maybe It Did.

Mattie Silks was one of the leading madams of the Old West. She had brothels in Dodge City, Kansas, Springfield, Illinois, plus several in Colorado including Georgetown and Denver.

Katie Fulton was also a madam. She came to Denver just a few months before Mattie Silks. Some say she resented Silks' success. Others say she became a romantic rival to Silks' long-time boyfriend, Cortez D. Thomson.

In any event, one fine day, these two madams put on a display in the streets of Denver that is still talked about today: the infamous Nude Duel.

On August 24, 1877, Mattie Silks squared off with Katie Fulton at the Olympic Gardens in downtown Denver. Both women were armed with pistols. They stood facing each other, raised their weapons, and fired.

Oh, wait. Before they opened fire, they stripped off their upper clothes. They were bare to their waists. Then they opened fire on each other.

Neither woman was struck, but a bystander was wounded by

one of the stray bullets. The duel was over, and everybody went home.

Mattie Silks

Now, what would cause two women to do naked gunfighting? Why, it was a man, of course. Cortez Thomson was Mattie Silks' man. Katie Fulton wanted him. So they decided that a naked duel was the way to settle the disagreement. It almost ended it permanently.

Remember the poor bystander that was struck by one of the misdirected shots? Well, that was Cortez Thomson. The two madams were fighting over him, and they almost killed him in their bloodlust. This goes down in history as one of the wackiest gunfights in the Old West, and maybe in the entire world.

Well, that's the story that is still being told today. The only trouble with it is that it never happened. Oh, sure, there was trouble between the two women, and there was a bit of physical violence, but there wasn't a duel. And nobody was walking around half naked waving guns. That was all the product of the imaginative pen of Forbes Parkhill, a writer born in 1892, long after the supposed duel. Parkhill first wrote about the duel around 1950. His titillating account was much more interesting than the true facts.

Nonetheless, Parkhill's account is false. Every bit of it, except for the date of the incident. He even got the names wrong. Katie Fulton was never known as Katie. She was called Kate. Cortez D. Thomson did tend to spell his name various ways, but never as "Coreze." He commonly went by the nickname Cort.

The name changes are pretty minor. Parkhill got all the important facts wrong too. The two women were not naked to the waist. They were full clothed. They did not duel. Neither of them shot Thomson.

The one kernel of truth to Parkhill's entire story is that Thomson did get shot. Nobody knows who did it, but we do know who didn't. It was an unidentified man; not either of the women.

The true story may not have the sexual aspect of naked fighting, but it is a very interesting example of the cold, hard life of the Old West. Ladies didn't always act like ladies; and gentlemen didn't always act like gentlemen. Sometimes they were animals.

Hang on. Here come the facts.

Mattie Silks was one of the most successful of Old West madams. She was known as the Queen of the Red Light District in Denver. She lived a life of luxury and excessive spending. She took it in fast, and she spent it fast. When she died, she left a few thousand dollars in jewelry and real estate.

Kate (not Katie) Fulton was a competing madam in Denver. Just like in today's world, the two madams had no reason to be friends and every reason to be enemies. They didn't need a no-account deadbeat like Cortez Thomson to raise their tempers. He was Silks' boyfriend, and Fulton wasn't interested in interfering.

If Fulton wanted a man to cheat her, beat her, and steal her money, there were plenty of others in Denver to fit that bill. Thomson and his bad temper and bad habits was solely the boyfriend of Silks. He was well known for mistreating Silks and stealing her money. It didn't seem to matter to her. She stayed with him through thick and thin.

On August 24, 1877, two drunken madams, Silks and Fulton, were sloppily arguing at Denver Park. They got loud with each other, but they weren't physical. Cort Thomson stepped between them. He said he was there to protect Silks and promptly punched Fulton smack dab in the face.

That didn't go down very well with the crowd. A man named Samuel Thatcher stepped up and tried to defend Fulton. Thomson smacked him in the face too.

At this point, Thomson's friends in the bar came to his aid. They tried to get to Thatcher, but they were stopped by Fulton. She pleaded with them to leave Thatcher alone. Thomson wasn't to be stopped though. He kicked Fulton square in the face, shattering her nose. Blood streamed down her face.

Thomson wasn't done. He attempted to draw his gun, but he was quickly disarmed. That pretty much ended the fight, but not the hard feelings. Thomson had punched and kicked Kate Fulton in the face and then tried to shoot her. Not everyone was forgiving.

That night, while returning home by carriage, an unidentified man ran up and fired a single shot at Thomson. It grazed his neck with a minor wound. Thomson didn't return fire, and the man ran off into the darkness never to be seen again.

Kate Fulton left Denver for Kansas City on the morning train. Speculation has it that she was uncertain whether she would be arrested by the Denver Police, even though she was attacked viciously by Cort Thomson. That may have been a smart move. A few days later, Mattie Silks filed a complaint with the District Attorney alleging threats made by Kate Fulton. Nothing ever grew out of the charges as Fulton never returned to Colorado.

And that is the true story of the Silks-Fulton Nude Duel.

JONATHAN R. DAVIS AND THE SYDNEY DUCKS

The Ducks Thought They Had a Pigeon

Jonathan Davis was an honorable man, living a fairly uneventful life. His greatest claim to fame was his injury in the Battle of Churubusco during the Mexican-American War. He was a captain in the Palmetto Regiment of Volunteers, and he was one of 865 American wounded during that August 20, 1847, battle. 133 were killed that day. The Mexicans suffered twice the number of deaths, but half the number of wounded. The Americans won the battle and captured over 1,800. When the war was over, Davis returned to civilian life.

The Battle of Churubusco by J. Cameron

The Sydney Ducks were a San Francisco gang. Many of them were once prisoners in the Australian penal colonies. Others had migrated to Australia following the Great Irish Famine and then migrated again to the San Francisco area. Sydney was the largest city in Australia, and they adopted it as part of their name.

The Ducks were an awful gang, involved in just about all forms of crime. They originally based their operations near Telegraph Hill in San Francisco. They called it Sydney Town. Later when they grew large enough to terrorize the entire city, Sydney Town became famous as the Barbary Coast. Laws did not matter to them. They robbed and killed at will.

And one day, Jonathan Davis met the Sydney Ducks on a lonely miner's trail near Sacramento, California. The Ducks met their match that day.

To be fair, of the thirteen men that attacked Davis and his friends, only five of them were known as Sydney Ducks. The rest were just as disreputable though. They were a bloodthirsty crew, and they liked their work.

The Ducks had been working the area lately. Miners were easy pickings. They weren't well armed, and they often had money or gold. The gang had killed ten miners in the past few days. They killed four miners the day before, and six Chinese miners the day before that. They were looking for more.

Captain Davis was a miner without a mine. He hadn't staked a claim yet. That was the purpose of his present trip. He was looking for an unclaimed place that would be easy to mine. Traveling with him were his two partners: James McDonald, and a local doctor, Bolivar Sparks.

The bandits attacked them in a narrow pass near Rocky-Canon. It was a deep gorge and a perfect place for a surprise ambush. McDonald was killed before he could unholster his weapon. Dr. Sparks managed to get off a few shots before he went down in a hail of bullets. He wasn't dead, but he wasn't moving either.

That left only Davis. He was well armed with two pistols and his Bowie knife. He wasn't about to back down. Davis advanced on the bandits and began firing. The outlaws found that they could not retreat. The narrow pass that they used to set up their ambush had turned into a killing field.

Davis emptied both pistols. Of his 12 shots, he killed 7 of the 13 bandits. Six were still alive, and their pistols were as empty as his. Reloading was time consuming, and there was no time. Davis advanced on the men with his Bowie knife. They attacked with their knives. One had a sword. Davis slashed and stabbed. In short order, four of the six lay dead on the ground. The last two bandits fled the area.

All of this happened in plain view of a group of miners who were out hunting. From their vantage point, they saw the three miners coming down the path, and they saw the bandits jump out and attack them. They came running down and helped Captain Davis tend to the injured Dr. Sparks. The miners made sure the bandits were dead, and they buried them right there.

There were unconfirmed reports of several dozen bullet holes in Captain Davis's hat and clothes. That sounds a bit excessive and is probably stretching the truth. Davis was reputed to have suffered two very minor wounds, but there is no word as to whether they were bullet or knife wounds.

Davis walked out of the mountains carrying Dr. Sparks. They made it to the doctor's home, but he lived only a few days before succumbing to his wounds. Captain Davis gave his widow several hundred dollars in gold and paper money that the miners had taken off the bodies of the bandits.

Davis told his story around town. Initially, he was met with disbelief, but the miners backed up his story. The best proof was the 11 shallow graves of the bandits, and the one properly dug grave of his partner, James McDonald.

There is no reliable evidence of the length of the fight. Some say it was a very short two minutes. That's very possible. The bandits became caught in their own trap. They were crowded together in tight quarters.

Davis advanced to where they were hiding and shot them down. The remaining men were right in front him when he and the bandits both ran out of bullets. When they attacked with their knives, they didn't have to chase him down. He was standing among them.

After the attack, Captain Davis went about his peaceful business and faded away into the sunset, as the cowboys are apt to say. Records have been dug up showing that he paid taxes, was counted in a census, and applied for a veteran's pension; so we know that he lived to become fairly old. He faded away completely after he applied for that pension. He would have been 71 at that time. I like to think he had another couple of decades left in him. But no one knows, and no one ever will.

JOHN WESLEY HARDIN

A Man Who Really Liked
His Peace and Quiet

John Wesley Hardin was a rascal. In fact, he was a rascal's rascal. Well, if you can call a cold-blooded murderer, thief, and bandit a rascal, then Hardin was a rascal.

Never a man to tell the same story the same way twice, Hardin embellished, contradicted, and stretched the truth about his exploits with abandon. Despite being one of the most prolific killers in the West, Hardin is most famous for the time he killed a man for snoring. Or was it a half dozen men? Or none at all? Ask Hardin about it on three consecutive days, and you might have get three different answers.

Here are the facts as understood by most people, but not necessarily Hardin. John Wesley Hardin was born on May 26, 1853, the son of a Methodist traveling preacher. He was hot-headed and belligerent from his early days. He tried to join the Confederate Army at 9. He almost killed a fellow student in a knife fight at 14. In 1868, at age 15, he killed his first man, Maje Holshousen, a former slave of his uncle.

John Wesley Hardin

From this young age, Hardin was an outlaw constantly on the run. He would spend the next 9 years as a wanted man. Hardin claimed to have killed 42 men. He certainly killed more than his share, but some of his claims are outright lies and others cannot be proved. He is given "credit" for 27 deaths. The true number is probably higher.

After he went on the run, the deaths started piling up. Everywhere he went, he seemed to run into a fight, a posse, a drunk, a bandit, etc., and somebody (or two or three) would end up dead. Hardin fought with just about anybody. He had no respect for the law, the Army, or innocent citizens. No respect. None at all.

> *I waylaid them, as I had no mercy on men whom I*
> *knew only wanted to get my body to torture and kill.*
> *It was war to the knife for me, and I brought it on*
> *by opening the fight with a double-barreled shotgun*
> *and ended it with a cap and ball six-shooter. Thus it*
> *was by the fall of 1868 I had killed four men and was*
> *myself wounded in the arm. John Wesley Hardin*

And then he met Wild Bill Hickok. Hardin seemed to respect Hickok, but that didn't keep him from dangerously testing Hickok. Hardin had been in Abilene, Kansas, long enough to make a few friends. At the time, he was known as Wesley Clemmons and/or Little Arkansaw.

Hardin was friendly with the owners of the Bull's Head Tavern, and they had had a disagreement with Hickok. That may be why Hickok confronted Hardin that night and demanded his guns. It was a violation to wear them in town. Hardin handed over his guns, but he taught Wild Bill a dangerous lesson that could have ended in the death of one or both of them.

Hardin slowly pulled his pistols from their holsters and held them out to Hickok. He held them "butt first" with the barrels pointed back at himself. Suddenly, with a flick of his wrist, he turned both guns around and held them on Hickok for a second. Then he handed .them over.

They must have become friends of a sort because Hardin came through Abilene a short time later and Hickok allowed him to keep his pistols. That was quite a break from Hickok's policy of no guns within the city limits. It also set the scene for one of the most unusual of murders. A murder, not of lust, greed, jealousy, or anger, but one of callous disregard for human life.

On August 6, 1871, Hardin rode into Abilene with his cousin, Gip Clements, and a friend named Charles Couger. They were rowdy and boisterous, spending the night drinking and gambling. Then they went to the American House Hotel to sleep it off. Hardin and his cousin were in one room. Couger slept alone in the adjoining room. The hotel had thin walls. It was easy to overhear a conversation in another room.

Couger snored. Oh,golly, did he snore. Hardin, in the next room, couldn't sleep for all the noise. He yelled for Couger to stop. He pounded on the walls to wake him. Couger would not wake up. The snoring continued.

Exasperated, Hardin pulled his pistols and fired through the walls twice. One bullet struck Couger in the head killing him instantly.

*"Roll over." John Wesley Hardin before he
shot Charles Couger for snoring*

The noise woke up the hotel, and they soon discovered the dead man. Hardin grabbed what clothes he could and jumped out the window with his cousin. Hickok was running up the stairs with four deputies at the same time. Hardin and his cousin galloped off into the night never to return to Abilene again.

*"They tell lots of lies about me. They say I killed six
or seven men for snoring. Well, it ain't true. I only
killed one man for snoring." John Wesley Hardin*

On another occasion, he claimed that he didn't kill a snoring man that night. Instead, according to Hardin, he killed a thief who was trying to make off with his pants.

Hardin would remain free until August 24, 1877 when he was captured in Pensacola, Florida. For a man who lived by the gun, he made a very amateurish mistake. When he was accosted by the officers, his pistol got caught in his suspenders.

Hardin was sentenced to 25 years in prison, but he was released in 1894 after serving 17 years. He was only 40 years old. Within a year, he was shot in the back of the head by John Selman, Sr. Hardin fell to the floor, and Selman fired three more shots into his body.

Selman plead self-defense at his first trial. It ended with a hung jury. Before the second trial started, he was killed in a shootout with US Marshal George Scarborough.

John Wesley Hardin is buried in the Concordia Cemetery in El Paso, Texas. He was a colorful figure in his time, but he brought death and pain with him everywhere he went.

"If you wish to be successful in life, be temperate

*and control your passions; if you don't, ruin and
death is the result." John Wesley Hardin*

STAGECOACH MARY

More Woman Than You Can Handle;
More Man Than You'll Ever Be

Mary Fields was a hard-drinking, foul-mouthed brawler with a short temper and a long memory. Mary Fields was a good-hearted, charitable, hard-working woman loved by everyone.

Both of those statements are true. Mary was rough around the edges in more ways than one, but she had a big heart. Those who knew her loved her.

Mary stood about six-foot tall and weighed a good 200 pounds or more. She wore a 38 Smith and Wesson on her hip, men's work clothes, drank like a fish, and smoked a cigar. She was a sight to behold.

She wasn't mean, though. On the contrary, she was good-natured and generous to a fault. Cascade, Montana, her home in her later years, actually closed the schools on her birthday. Rough and tumble Mary won the hearts of men, women and children through her amiable personality and goodwill.

And of course, she drove a stagecoach.

No. No, she didn't. That was just her nickname. In truth, she would have had an easier time if she drove a stagecoach.

Mary Fields was born into slavery in Hickman County, Tennessee, around 1832. She was freed in 1865 at the conclusion of the Civil War when slavery was outlawed in the United States.

For a time, she worked on Mississippi River steamboats. Then she met Judge Edmund Dunne, future Chief Justice of the Arizona Supreme Court. She worked for the Dunne family, tending to their five children and the housekeeping. In 1883, Josephine Dunne, the mother, died, and the family moved to Toledo, Ohio, to be near Judge Dunne's sister, Mother Mary Amadeus, the Mother Superior of an Ursuline convent.

The next year, Mother Amadeus was sent to Montana to open a school for Native American girls. She took sick with pneumonia, and Mary went west to take care of her. Mother Amadeus recovered, and Mary took a permanent job at the school. She did all the jobs from growing vegetables to carpentry to freight delivery.

She did so well that she was made foreman. That led to trouble. White males at the school didn't like begin ordered around by a black woman. Word were exchanged. It became physical. Someone knocked her down. Mary produced a gun and fired off a few shots. And that was that. Mary was ordered to leave.

It didn't end her friendship with Mother Amadeus. She helped Mary open a restaurant in Cascade. She was a good cook, and she kept a clean establishment, but she went broke in less than a year. Kind-hearted Mary's downfall was giving away food to the poor and homeless.

Mary Fields, better known as Stagecoach Mary

Her next job was mail delivery. This is where she got her nickname, Stagecoach Mary. She didn't work for the United States Post Office. She won a contract to deliver the mail for them. She didn't use a stagecoach either. She had a wagon and her faithful mule, Moses. Her mail was delivered on time. When the Montana snow became too deep for the wagon, she put on her snowshoes and did it that way. Stagecoach Mary got the job done.

Mary was about 60 years old when she began delivering mail. She got the job by proving she was more capable than the other applicants. She did that by showing her skill in hitching up horses. When she won the first contract, she became the second woman and the first African American to work for the Post Office. She did two four-year contracts and then retired to open up a laundry in her home and a babysitting service.

"She drinks whiskey, and she swears, and she
is a republican, which makes her a low, foul
creature." Unknown Schoolgirl Class Essay

Stagecoach Mary was a sweet-natured woman. She was well liked by everyone, despite her rougher qualities. The Cascade schools really did close on her birthdays. They loved her and her rough ways. They weren't alone in their admiration. When Montana passed a law making it illegal for a woman to enter a saloon, the mayor of Cascade granted her an exemption.

Her enemies were few and far between, but she did have a few. She was outspoken and not afraid to argue with words or fists. One day while drinking her lunch in a local saloon, she saw a man who refused to pay his laundry bill. She ran outside, spun the man around, and broke his nose. "His debt is now paid," she yelled.

Mary wasn't greedy. If the man was unable to pay, she would

have written off his bill. She did that when she ran her restaurant, and she did it with her laundry and daycare. They say she
spent most of her money buying candy and gifts for the children
in the town.

The famous actor, Gary Cooper, was one of her fans. He met
her at the age of nine. He grew up in Helena, Montana, and he
knew all about Mary. Ebony Magazine interviewed him in 1959,
and he went on and on with stories about her. She was, and still
is, a legend in Montana.

*"Born a slave somewhere in Tennessee, Mary
lived to become one of the freest souls ever to
draw a breath, or a .38." Actor Gary Cooper*

ONE-EYED CHARLIE

*The First Woman to Vote in a
Presidential Election in California*

Charlotte Darkey Parkhurst, aka One-Eyed Charley, Six-Horse Charley, Cockeyed Charley or plain ol' Charley was born a woman, but mostly lived as a man. She was born in in Sharon, Vermont, in 1812 and ended up in an orphanage in New Hampshire. She ran away at the age of 12 and took up work as a stablehand, a male stablehand.

Female Charley told everyone that he was an orphan. He was, of course. What he didn't say was that he was a woman. He probably wouldn't have gotten his job in the stables if he did. From this point, Charley lived the rest of his life as a man. He called himself a man, and that is how he will be referred to in the rest of this story.

Charley was a natural with horses. He learned to care for them, ride them, hitch them up and drive them.

Charley spent quite a few years back East working in Rhode Island, Massachusetts, and some long routes up and down the East Coast. He was in his 30s when he decided to travel to California. They say he might have gotten the idea from James E. Birch, another stagecoach driver. Birch went west and started a one-wagon freight service that grew into the largest California stage line, the California Stage Company.

*Plaque in Soquel, California fire station where
Charley Parkhurst voted (if she did)*

Oddly enough, Charley didn't travel overland, even though he probably could have found ready employment driving freight west. Instead he took a steamer to Panama and another ship to California. On the way, he met John Morton who owned a drayage which is a short-haul freight service. Charley became one of his drivers. Sometime in his employment, Charley lost an eye due to a kick in the head from a horse. That led to his nicknames of One-Eyed Charley and Cockeyed Charley.

Later on, he took a job with James Birch and his growing stagecoach line. Charley rapidly became one of his best drivers. This is where he earned the nickname Six-Horse Charley for his expertise with large coaches and wagons.

He also earned the nickname Whip which is a term used to identify a top driver. He ranked among the best in the West. One of them, Hank Monk, was involved in a humorous incident with Horace Greeley.

Like Charley, Monk started working in stables as a preteen back East and then moved to California where he also worked for James E. Birch and the California Stage Company among other stage lines.

One day, Monk had one passenger, Horace Greeley, on his run to Placerville. Greeley mentioned that he needed to make it to a lecture on time. Monk let him settle in and then set off at a fast pace.

The road they were on was well traveled, but it certainly

wasn't smooth and flat. Greeley bounced up and down. Legend has it that the buttons popped off his coat one by one as he was slammed around in the back of the coach. That wasn't the worst of it. At one point, Greeley's head crashed through the roof of the coach whereupon he yelled to Monk that he wasn't in as much of a hurry as he was a while ago. Monk said, "Keep your seat, Horace, and I'll get you there on time."

That story reeks of embellishment, but there is probably a kernel of truth in it. In any event, Hank Monk was one of the best, and Charley was his equal. He just didn't have a humorous story. He made up for it with his colorful nicknames.

Charley continued to drive stagecoaches until the railroads were built. There really weren't that many stagecoach robberies when one considers the number of stage lines and stagecoaches, but Charley is credited with killing at least one unlucky bandit.

After he retired as a driver, he lived around Watsonville, California, doing a bit of farming and lumbering. He suffered from rheumatism and tongue cancer. On December 18, 1879, One-Eyed Charley died peacefully in his sleep.

Soquel, California, Post Office mural proclaiming One-Eyed Charley as the first woman to vote in a presidential election in California

Charley knew his time was coming. He had made arrangements with his friends to do certain things for him after he passed away. They came to his cabin with a doctor and helped lay out his body for burial. It was then that his secret was discovered. Charley was a female.

Even more astounding was the doctor's conclusion that Charley had give birth at some time. People were amazed. No one had ever doubted that Six-Horse Charley was a male, and yet here was absolute proof.

Charley's friends went through his belongings as per his wishes. They came upon a baby's dress. Nothing was found as to the identity of the father or what happened to the baby.

The newspapers had a field day with the story. Charley was well known from his stagecoach days. His obituary was carried throughout the country from East to West.

"Thirty Years in Disguise: A Noted Old Californian Stage-Driver Discovered after Death to be a Woman." Headline of the San Francisco Call

Charley would have faded into history along with Hank Monk and the rest of the stagecoach drivers, except for one tiny bit of seemingly mundane evidence. Charley registered to vote in the national election of 1868. There is no record that he actually voted, but it is assumed that he did. As such Charley became the first Californian woman to vote in a presidential election.

Charley has been the subject of a large handful of books, articles, TV shows and lectures. No one can say for sure what his sexual orientation truly was, but there has been a lot of speculation. All we know is Charley was born a female and lived the majority of his life as a male, but somewhere along the way he gave birth to at least one child.

Headstone of One-Eyed Charley Parkhurst,
Watsonville, California

No matter how one chooses to view his sexual life, One-Eyed Charley, one of the best whips in stagecoach history, led an honorable and distinguished life. He was a legend among legends. He deserves to be remembered for his outstanding work as a driver, rather than merely for whether he/she voted in an election.

Ride on, Charley. Ride on.

"He was in his day one of the most dexterous and celebrated of the famous California drivers ranking with Foss, Hank Monk, and George Gordon, and it was an honor to be striven for to occupy the spare end of the driver's seat when the fearless Charley Parkhurst held the reins of a four-or six-in hand...

"Last Sunday [December 28, 1879], in a little cabin on the Moss Ranch, about six miles from Watsonville, Char-

ley Parkhurst, the famous coachman, the fearless fighter, the industrious farmer and expert woodman died of the cancer on her tongue. She knew that death was approaching, but she did not relax the reticence of her later years other than to express a few wishes as to certain things to be done at her death. Then, when the hands of the kind friends who had ministered to her dying wants came to lay out the dead body of the adventurous Argonaut, a discovery was made that was literally astounding. Charley Parkhurst was a woman." Obituary of Charley Parkhurst, the San Francisco Call

ANNIE OAKLEY

Secret Weapon of the US Army

(Almost)

Annie was one of the best marksmen of her time. Almost all who write about her say that she was one of the best FEMALE sharpshooters, but that is doing her an injustice. She was remarkable. The things she could do were hard to duplicate. Even the best would be hard pressed to equal her.

She learned to shoot because she needed to shoot. She hunted and trapped for a living from her time as a child to her early adulthood.

She was born as Phoebe Ann Mosey (or Moses) in Darke County, Ohio, on August 13, 1860, to a large family. She was the sixth of nine children. When her father, Jacob Mosey, died, she was six. The family struggled with poverty. Her mother, Susan Wise Mosey, remarried, but soon became a widow once more.

At the age of 10, Annie was hired by a local couple to be a live-in caregiver for their son. It was not a pleasant time. She endured physical and mental abuse. One story she told was of being forced out into a freezing night without shoes. Why? Because she fell asleep while darning socks. Annie never identified the couple in her autobiography or interviews. She referred to them as "the wolves."

Phoebe Ann Mosey aka Annie Oakley

She ran away from "the wolves" at age 12, and she returned to her mother's home at age 15. Annie started trapping when she was just six years old. She was hunting by age eight. It put food on the table, and the excess brought in needed money. She was well known to the cooks and chefs at the restaurants and hotels in the area.

When she returned to her mother, her hunting skills helped them pay off the mortgage on their farm. More than that, her reputation was growing in her area of Ohio. It grew so much that when traveling marksman Frank E. Butler came to Cincinnati with his Baughman & Butler traveling show, a local hotel owner bet Butler $100 that Annie could best him.

"I was eight years old when I made my first
shot, and I still consider it one of the best shots
I ever made." Annie Oakley describing how
she shot a squirrel off her front porch.

She did. It was a heck of a display by both shooters with Butler losing on the 25th and final shot. Butler was enraptured by Miss Oakley, and he began courting her. They married a year later.

The story is true, but there is a lot of confusion as to exactly where the shooting match took place and when it took place. It may have occurred in 1875 or as late as 1881. There are various explanations. A likely one is that Annie was often intentionally billed as being younger than she was.

At any rate, Frank Butler married the young Phoebe Ann Mosey. They settled in Cincinnati. This is where she adopted the name Annie Oakley. A local neighborhood was called Oakley. Annie never said, but that's possibly where she got the name.

In 1885, at the age of 25, they joined Buffalo Bill's Wild West Show. She quickly became a headliner. Her showstopper was shooting a card in half from 30 yards. She would do it multiple times until there wasn't enough of the card left to shoot at.

She didn't cheat or use tricks. She was really that good. She was so well known and respected that the German Emperor Kaiser Wilhelm allowed her to shoot a cigar from his mouth. She also performed for Queen Victoria of England, King Umberto of Italy, and other heads of state.

Buffalo Bill's Wild West poster featuring Annie Oakley

Sitting Bull, legendary leader of the Hunkpapa Lakotas, gave her the nickname "Watanya Cicilla" which translated to "Little Sure Shot." Sitting Bull was part of the show for a short time, but he met Annie before that. He was a fan. When he met her, he insisted on adopting her. As part of the adoption, he affectionately named her Watanya Cicilla. Annie loved the name and loved Sitting Bull.

Annie was also a nice person. She was known for donating to charity. She donated her time to teach women how to handle weapons. Some say she taught up to 15,000 women.

Annie Oakley shooting behind her using a mirror

As nice as she was, she wasn't a pushover by any means. William Randolph Hearst, the newspaper magnate, found that out the hard way. In 1903, two of his newspapers reported that Annie was arrested for shoplifting to pay for her cocaine habit. Annie vowed to clear her name. She sued a whopping 55 newspapers that carried the story. She won 54 of those lawsuits, including the ones against Hearst's newspapers.

"I would like to see every woman know how

*to handle guns as naturally as they know
how to handle babies." Annie Oakley*

When the Spanish American War came along in 1898, Annie stepped forward once again. Following in the footsteps of Teddy Roosevelt and the Rough Riders, she organized a team of 50 sharpshooters. All of them were women. Sadly, the Army turned them away. Had the Army been more progressive in their thinking, Annie surely would have earned her place in history as a military leader. Perhaps we would know her as Colonel Annie and the Sure Shots. That would be fitting. When the Rough Riders stormed San Juan Hill, I am positive they would have welcomed Annie's band of 50 crack shots.

Annie Oakley at age 62

Free passes to movies or shows often had punch marks to distinguish them from paid tickets. People called them Annie Oakleys because they were similar to the playing cards that Annie would shoot full of holes in her act.

Annie Oakley has a well-deserved reputation as a hunter, trapper, woodsman, and marksman. She headlined Buffalo Bill's Wild West Show for years. She was adopted by the great Lakota leader Sitting Bull.

She was the absolute epitome of a rooting-tooting, self-sufficient independent woman of the West, but in truth, her only connection with the West was exhibition dates with Buffalo Bill. The farthest West she ever lived was Ohio.

She was an Easterner, but boy, oh boy, did she act like she was from the Old West.

Oakley playfully skipped on stage, lifted her rifle, and aimed the barrel at a burning candle. In one shot, she snuffed out the flame with a whizzing bullet. Sitting Bull watched her knock corks off of bottles and slice through a cigar Butler held in his teeth." R. A. Koestler-Grack

NED CHRISTIE'S WAR

The Fugitive Who Just Went Home

The story of Ned Christie is one of a murderous outlaw relentlessly pursued. Or perhaps it is one of an innocent man hounded to his death. We know almost all of his story, but no one really knows whether he committed the crime that started it all.

Ned Christie or NeDe WaDe (Ned, Son of Watt), was a tribal leader of the Cherokee Nation. His father, Watt, and his grandfather, Lacy, were also leaders at one time. He was a strong, tall man at 6 feet 4 inches with the hardened body of a blacksmith.

Two notable events occurred in 1885, two years before the first incidents in Ned Christie's War. The first was that Ned was elected to the Cherokee Senate. The second was that he was tried in the tribal courts and found not guilty of manslaughter in the death of William Palone. Palone, also Cherokee, had allegedly insulted Ned's mother.

Ned Christie, born NeDe WaDe

Add in that Ned was a hot head known for frequently drinking to excess, and you have the gist of the arguments for and against his guilt in the 1887 incident that started Ned Christie's War. One side said Ned was falsely charged in order to remove him from the Cherokee Senate. The other side said Ned was a carousing drunk who had killed in the past.

The incidents leading to the War really didn't concern Christie at first. US Deputy Marshal Daniel Maples and his posse were searching for Bill Pigeon, an outlaw, whiskey peddler, and suspected murderer of a deputy. They didn't find Pigeon, but they did run into an ambush.

Maples and another man, George Jefferson, were heading back to their camp when shots were fired at them near Tahlequah, Oklahoma. Maples was struck. He died the next day.

The shooter was not seen, but the other men in the posse suspected that it was Bud Trainor (or Trainer). Trainor was also a known whiskey trader. The posse started rounding up Trainor's friends. One of them, John Parris, was also Ned Christie's friend. Parris told the marshals that Christie was the culprit.

Christie was in the area. In fact, some say he was drinking with Parris the night before. The day after the shooting, Christie was walking towards Tahlequah when he met a friend who told him he was wanted for murdering Marshal Maples.

Christie turned around and headed home. He talked to his father and his friends about the situation. Watt Christie told his son to turn himself in. His friends thought he should run. Ned did neither. Instead, he went home and stayed there. The home he went to was a cabin in a remote section of Indian Territory. He brought his wife and her son with him.

He didn't trust the US courts to give him a fair trial. According to some stories, Christie wrote to Judge Isaac Parker (the famous hanging judge). He said that he would surrender if Parker would put him on bail so he could look for evidence. If Parker ever received such a letter, we will never know, but we do know that he never responded.

What Judge Parker did do was send a series of marshals to arrest Christie. For five years, they chased him, shot him, burned him, but did not catch him.

Heck Thomas, one of the famous marshals known as the Three Guardsmen, was sent by Parker in 1889. He was accompanied by several other marshals and Bud Trainor. They found his house, and they had a shootout. Christie held them off until they burned his house to the ground. He wasn't caught, but he did take a bullet in the gunfight.

Marshal Henry "Heck" Thomas

Christie, with his house burned down, went deeper into isolated territory. He built a better cabin near Wauhillau. This cabin is referred to as Ned's Fort. It was built to withstand an attack. It had double walls and built-in slits for rifles.

Christie still wasn't hiding. He wasn't surrendering, but he wasn't running either. He simply lived his life. Marshals and posses kept coming after him. At first, he was able to hold them off. There were a couple of times that marshals were wounded during these attacks. Christie felt he was simply defending himself against unjust attacks. The marshals, of course, felt differently.

In 1892, a military-style assault was planned. The posse consisted of 16 men led by Deputy Gideon "Cap" White, a former Cavalry chaptain. White convinced the Army to lend him a cannon. Previous attempts to capture Christie had been foiled by his extra-strong cabin. They intended to blow up the cabin if he wouldn't surrender.

On the morning of November 3, 1892, Ned Christie woke up

to calls for his surrender. He did not do so immediately, and rifle fire peppered the cabin. No harm was done, but Christie called for a truce to remove his wife and children. The posse allowed them to leave.

They gave Christie an ultimatum: surrender or die. Christie refused to give up. Deputy White ordered the cannon to be fired. It struck the cabin, but didn't do much damage. They fired again and again and again. Reportedly, they fired a whopping 38 cannon balls at Ned Christie's cabin and thousands of bullets without causing substantial damage. Ned was still free and still resisting.

Deputy White ordered his men to fire again, but this time, he had them use double the powder. When they set it off, it certainly caused a lot more damage than the earlier shots. It destroyed the cannon – and caused no harm to the cabin.

The posse was frustrated. They decided to use dynamite. Some say they pushed a wagon load of it against one of the walls. Others say they constructed a crude wooden shield to allow them to get close and then toss several sticks of dynamite at the cabin. The second choice is probably the true one.

Poor Ned. His "fort" was able to withstand a concerted attack by over a dozen men and a cannon, but it couldn't hold up to dynamite. They blew half of it away, and the rest was on fire. He had no choice. He had to come out.

And come out he did. Not to give up, but to continue the fight. Ned charged at the posse with a gun in each hand. They quickly cut him down. Ned Christie had fought his final battle.

The posse took the body to authorities in Fort Smith, Arkansas, to confirm the kill and get their bounty. Afterwards, the body was released to the family. Ned was buried in Wauhillau at the Watt Christie Cemetery.

26 years later, a man named Dick Humphreys testified to the killing of Marshal Maples. He said that he saw the shooting. According to Humphreys, one of the original suspects, Bud Trainor, was the real killer. Humphreys said he kept quiet for over a quarter of a century out of fear of retribution from Trainor.

Was Ned Christie innocent? Maybe. He didn't act like a criminal. He just stayed home and defended himself when the marshals and posses came for him. Some say he was killed because he was on the opposing side of some issues in the tribal Senate.

Was Ned Christie guilty? Maybe. He had been charged with manslaughter in an earlier case, and he was well-known for being loud and argumentative. He was in the area at the time of the murder, and he refused to surrender for trial.

A growing number of researchers argue for his innocence. This author concurs with that opinion.

Members of the posse that killed Ned Christie posing with his corpse in November 1892. 1) Paden Tolbert 2) Capt G.S White; 3) Coon Ratteree 4) Enoch Mills 5) Ned Christie {deceased}; 6) Thomas Johnson 7) Charles Copeland 8) Heck Bruner

DYNAMITE DAN CLIFTON

The Most Killed

Outlaw in America

Dynamite Dan, aka Dynamite Dick, lived to be 31, but he died many times. The last one was permanent.

Dan lived in Oklahoma. During his short life, he was a pretty bad man. He earned his nickname because he knew how to crack a safe. He was a stick-up man when he wasn't doing a big job. He even rustled some cattle.

Then he met the Doolin Gang. The Doolin Gang was closely related to the Dalton Gang. The leader of the Doolin's, Bill Doolin, had been in the Dalton's. One of the Dalton Brothers, Bill, was in the Doolin Gang.

Dynamite Dan became one of the eleven people in the gang. It was quite a vicious gang. They got started in 1892. By 1900, all but two of them were dead. All eleven met their deaths in gun-fights with the law.

The Doolin Gang was known by a number of names: the Doolin-Dalton Gang, the Oklahombres, the Oklahoma Long Riders, and the Wild Bunch. They were the original Wild Bunch before Butch Cassidy and the Sundance Kid.

Dynamite Dan was true to his name. He knew his dynamite, and that made him a valuable member of a gang that robbed banks and trains.

Being a member of an outlaw gang is dangerous, and Dan lost three of his fingers in Ingalls, Oklahoma, in 1893 during a gunfight with authorities. It wasn't dynamite. The fingers were shot off.

There are alternate stories about his fingers. Some say he lost them as a child while playing with dynamite or while trying to crack a safe.

At any rate, Dynamite Dan was missing three fingers, and because he was part of the Doolin Gang, he had a bounty of $3,500 on his head.

This led to people turning in bodies or photos purporting to be Dan. All of them showed men missing three fingers. None of them were missing the correct three fingers.

It's a mystery as to where these bodies came from. I suppose each sheriff, marshal or lawman figured that out for himself.

Can you imagine the possibilities?

Hey, Sheriff, I got Dynamite Dan.

No, you didn't. I have him here in my wagon.

Don't believe them, Sheriff. I brought three bodies just to be sure.

At any rate, Dynamite Dan joined the Doolin Gang in 1892 and was dead by 1896. He was shot dead by US Marshal Chris Madsen. He is buried in the Muskogee, Oklahoma, town cemetery.

That didn't stop people from bringing in bodies. It continued for years.

He was truly the "most killed outlaw in America."